ACTIVITIES FOR TEENS
77 Ways to Build Catholic Identity ❧ Ruth Puls

May · December · The Boat · Home Sweet Home · Christ Died for Me! · October · Witness! · January · Nov · March · Virtual Golf · Snow Globes · June · February · April · Story Art · Kites · September · Carving Out Your Life!

PFLAUM PUBLISHING GROUP
2621 Dryden Road • Dayton, OH 45439
Phone: 1-800-543-4383 • Fax 1-800-370-4450
Service@Pflaum.com • www.pflaum.com

ACTIVITIES FOR TEENS
77 Ways to Build Catholic Identity   Ruth Puls

Interior design by Patricia A. Lynch
Cover design by Larissa Thompson

©2002, Pflaum Publishing Group, Dayton, OH 45439 (800-543-4383) www.pflaum.com
All rights reserved. Permission to photocopy appropriate pages for use with participants in educational settings is granted to the buyer. The permission line must appear on each reproduced page. No other use of this text is granted without permission of the publisher.

The Scripture quotations contained herein are from the *New Revised Standard Version Bible*: Catholic Edition ©1993 and 1989 by the Division of Christian Education of the National Council of the Churches of Christ in the U.S.A. Used by permission. All rights reserved.

ISBN 0-937997-79-X
3214

DEDICATION

To my parents, who were my first and best teachers in faith.

ACKNOWLEDGMENTS

It is important to acknowledge the contributions of many people who helped to bring this project to completion. Special thanks goes to the young people of the Archdiocese of Baltimore who tested the discussion starters at a youth conference. Special thanks also to Susan, Ann Marie, Chris, Mark, Kevin, and Joanne of the youth ministry staff in Baltimore, who are always willing to listen to and critique an idea. The young people of the Church of the Resurrection in Ellicott City, Maryland, inspired many of the activities, and to them I am eternally grateful. Joanne Cahoon contributed **Story Art: Kites**, page 76, and some of the saints' biographies. She is a good colleague and an even better friend.

Most importantly, thanks goes to Sarah, JD, Steve, Gina, Brad, Genna, Brent, Sally, Jackie, Chris, and E.J., who make creating activities a way of life.

TABLE OF CONTENTS

Introduction 7

September

September-at-a-Glance 8
September from a Catholic Christian Perspective 8
Great Church Feast Days 8
Saint of the Month: St. Vincent de Paul 8
Catholic Jeopardy 9
The Boat 12
Baptism at the Movies 14
September Discussion Starter: The Radio Station 15

October

October-at-a-Glance 16
October from a Catholic Christian Perspective 16
Great Church Feast Days 16
Saint of the Month: St. Therese of Lisieux 16
Carving Out Your Life! 17
Home Sweet Home 20
Confirmation at the Movies 22
October Discussion Starter: The Convenience Store 23

November

November-at-a-Glance 24
November from a Catholic Christian Perspective 24
Great Church Feast Days 24
Saint of the Month: St. Martin de Porres 24
Remembrance Quilt 25
Who Wants To Be a Catholic Millionaire? 26
Eucharist at the Movies 28
November Discussion Starter: The Medical Test 28

December

December-at-a-Glance 30
December from a Catholic Christian Perspective 30
Great Church Feast Days 30
Saint of the Month: Our Lady of Guadalupe 30
Blessed Are the Peacemakers and the Piecemakers! 31
Witness! 33
Handout 1: Witness Questions 34
Reconciliation at the Movies 35
December Discussion Starter: The Parish Gift 35
Handout 2: Wish List 37

January

January-at-a-Glance 38
January from a Catholic Christian Perspective 38
Great Church Feast Days 38
Saint of the Month: St. John Bosco 38
Celebrating Our Holy Families 39
Handout 3: The Genealogy of Jesus Christ 40
Handout 4: Creating a Family Crest 41
Handout 5: Jesus' Family Tree 42
Anointing at the Movies 43
January Discussion Starter: The Park 44

February

February-at-a-Glance 45
February from a Catholic Christian Perspective 45
Saint of the Month: St. Blaise 45
Great Church Feast Days 46
Snow Globes 46
Handout 6: Making Snow Globes 47
Handout 7: Isaiah 1:18 48
Reconciliation: A Countercultural Idea 49
Handout 8: God's Word Speaks to Us 50
Handout 9: Answer Key 51
Matrimony at the Movies 52
February Discussion Starter: The Pharmacy 52

March

March-at-a-Glance 54
March from a Catholic Christian Perspective 54
Great Church Feast Days 54
Saint of the Month: St. Katharine Drexel 54
Feast of the Annunciation 55
Handout 10: The Birth Announcement—John the Baptist 56
Handout 11: The Birth Announcement—Jesus 57
Handout 12: A "Mom" Quiz for John the Baptist 58
Handout 13: A "Mom" Quiz for Jesus 59
Handout 14: Answer Key for the "Mom" Quizzes 60
A Lenten Challenge: Enter the Passion 61
Lenten Practice: Loving People, Not Things 62
Handout 15: The People of the Clan Potsontheground 63
March Discussion Starter: The Public Utility Company 66

April

April-at-a-Glance	68
April from a Catholic Christian Perspective	68
Great Church Feast Days	68
Saint of the Month: St. John Baptist de la Salle	68
Christ Died for Me!	69
Handout 16: Friend to the End	70
Looking at Resurrection Attitudes	71
Handout 17: Attitudes	72
Holy Orders at the Movies	73
April Discussion Starter: The Mayor's Office	73

May

May-at-a-Glance	75
May from a Catholic Christian Perspective	75
Great Church Feast Days	75
Saint of the Month: Saint Joseph	75
Story Art: Kites	76
Handout 18: Story Art Directions	78
Handout 19: The Spirit in Scripture	79
Virtual Golf	80
Handout 20: Virtual Golf Scorecard	81
May Discussion Starter: The Local Football Team	82

June

June-at-a-Glance	84
June from a Catholic Christian Perspective	84
Great Church Feast Days	84
Saint of the Month: John the Baptist	84
Rocks and Stones	85
Handout 21: Rocks and Stones	86
Handout 22: Rocks and Stones in Scripture	87
A Guided Meditation on Relationships	89
Handout 23: A Guided Meditation on Relationships	90
June Discussion Starter: The D.U.I. Arrest	92

INTRODUCTION

Sometimes young people are faulted for having too much energy. Actually their energy is a gift to us, and so is their enthusiasm. As adults, we are challenged to find ways to engage, embrace, and direct young people's energy and enthusiasm. We are challenged to help young people to use their gifts to build the reign of God.

This book of activities is intended to help adults meet the challenges of working with young people—from junior high through high school. It offers ways to engage young people in group situations. Following the academic year, the activities anticipate the month or the liturgical season. Background on the month, along with saints we honor that month, is there to spur your imagination.

In addition to activities, there is a discussion starter for each month. These discussion starters are intended to spark conversation. Young people are encouraged to be creative as they play the parts of characters who must make moral decisions in ripped-from-real-life situations. Then teens process the experience from a Catholic Christian perspective.

I hope that you find these activities helpful. I also hope that, as you find ways to engage the creativity and energy of young people, you will gain creativity and energy yourself. God bless you in your ministry to young people.

SEPTEMBER

SEPTEMBER-AT-A-GLANCE

Septem is Latin for seven, which was the seventh month of the Roman calendar. September is our ninth month, so we have a deviated *septem*.

SEPTEMBER FROM A CATHOLIC CHRISTIAN PERSPECTIVE

September is the month in which we celebrate the birth of Mary. It is the month of new beginnings, when young people, teachers, and administrators head back to school. It is a month when some of us wish we could roll back the calendar to the seventh month and have a couple more months of summer!

GREAT CHURCH FEAST DAYS

8 Birth of Blessed Virgin Mary—Everyone knows that Jesus' birthday is December 25. But did you know that this is his mother's birthday?

9 St. Peter Claver (d. 1654)—St. Peter Claver is known for helping slaves arriving in Cartagena, Colombia, from Africa.

13 St. John Chrysostom (d. 407)—The Church remembers St. John Chrysostom as a doctor, or accomplished teacher, of the Church.

14 Exaltation of the Holy Cross—This feast celebrates the discovery of relics of the true cross of Christ.

15 Our Lady of Sorrows—We commemorate the sorrows of the Blessed Virgin: the prophecy of Simeon, the flight into Egypt, the disappearance of the boy Jesus, the journey to Calvary, the crucifixion, and the burial of Jesus.

16 Sts. Cornelius (d. 253) and Cyprian (d. 258)—St. Cornelius, pope and martyr, is remembered along with his great supporter, St. Cyprian.

19 St. Januarius (d. 304)—The feast of this martyred bishop of Naples is celebrated on this day.

20 Sts. Andrew Kim Taegon (d. 1846) and Companions—St. Andrew Kim Taegon, the first native-born Korean priest, was martyred along with many other Korean Christians.

21 St. Matthew (first century)—The story of St. Matthew's conversion from tax collector to apostle is told in his own gospel.

SAINT OF THE MONTH
St. Vincent de Paul (1580-1660)

Born in 1580, St. Vincent de Paul grew up the son of poor parents, but because of his intelligence, he received a good education and was ordained a priest in 1600. Life's circumstances (he was captured by pirates and sold into slavery) and God's grace, as well as Vincent's own response to God's grace, led him to many works of charity. He made the choice to live among the poor.

Today we frequently think of someone who gives "charity" as looking down from above at persons with needs and then providing for those needs. Vincent first learned and then taught with his life and his words that charity was about loving God through loving others, particularly the poor. He founded a society of priests and co-founded the Daughters of Charity with St. Louise de Marillac. His life among and outreach to all in need—the poor and hungry,

CATHOLIC JEOPARDY

ON YOUR MARK!

- To enable young people to see how much they know and where they can grow in Catholic identity

orphans and widows—define him and are the reason St. Vincent is the patron saint of charitable societies. At the close of his life he professed to have done nothing. Ah, but God had done much!

St. Vincent de Paul's feast day is September 27.

GET SET!

- Make up an "answer board" with values attached. Assign points to each category.
- Have an appropriate award for the team that earns the most points.

Sample Answer Board

SACRAMENTS	DAYS OF THE WEEK	THE NAME GAME	IT'S IN THE BOOK	FINISH THIS STATEMENT
100	100	100	100	100
200	200	200	200	200
300	300	300	300	300
400	400	400	400	400
500	500	500	500	500

GO!

- Divide the group into teams of four.
- Ask each team to choose a spokesperson.
- Allow each group to choose a unique sound to signal that they know the question.
- The group with the most unique sound gets to start the game.
- This group has control of the board until they give a wrong question and another group signals that they have the right question. Please remember teens' responses must be in the form of questions!
- Explain that there will be only one round, with no "final jeopardy." Whoever has the most points at the end of this round, wins.
- If you do not want to keep track of points, award play money after each question.

CATHOLIC JEOPARDY ANSWERS AND QUESTIONS

CATEGORY: SACRAMENTS

POINTS	READ THIS ANSWER	TEENS GIVE YOU THIS QUESTION
100	Of three, seven, eleven, or twelve, this is the number of sacraments.	What is seven?
200	These three sacraments are called sacraments of initiation.	What are Baptism, Confirmation, and Eucharist?
300	These two sacraments are sacraments of healing.	What are Penance and Anointing of the Sick?
400	These two sacraments are concerned with lifestyle.	What are Matrimony and Holy Orders?
500	This mystery is the theme of every Mass.	What is the paschal mystery?

CATEGORY: DAYS OF THE WEEK

POINTS	READ THIS ANSWER	TEENS GIVE YOU THIS QUESTION
100	Easter is always on this day.	What is Sunday?
200	Pancake Tuesday is another name for this day.	What is Shrove Tuesday? or What is Mardi Gras?
300	Lent begins on this day.	What is Ash Wednesday?
400	The Feast of the Ascension falls forty days after Easter and is always on this day of the week.	What is Thursday?
500	This is the name of the Sunday before Easter.	What is Passion (or Palm) Sunday?

CATEGORY: THE NAME GAME

POINTS	READ THIS ANSWER	TEENS GIVE YOU THIS QUESTION
100	This word names both a Church leader and a bird.	What is a cardinal?
200	Capuchin monks gave us this drink.	What is cappuccino?
300	We use this same word for a piece on a chessboard and a member of the Church hierarchy.	What is a bishop?
400	This man was pope immediately prior to John Paul II.	Who is John Paul I?
500	Saul, persecutor of Christians, changed his name to this after his conversion.	Who is Paul?

CATEGORY: IT'S IN THE BOOK

POINTS	READ THIS ANSWER	TEENS GIVE YOU THIS QUESTION
100	These are the names of the four Gospels.	What are Matthew, Mark, Luke, and John?
200	The name of the first book of the Bible.	What is Genesis?
300	The name of the second book of the Bible.	What is Exodus?
400	Of these three—Mark, Peter, and Paul—this person does not lend his name to an epistle.	Who is Mark?
500	This person is referred to in the Scriptures as "the disciple Jesus loved."	Who is John?

CATEGORY: FINISH THIS STATEMENT

POINTS	READ THIS ANSWER	TEENS GIVE YOU THIS QUESTION
100	Christ has died, Christ has risen _____.	What comes before "Christ will come again"?
200	Blessed is the fruit _____.	What comes before "of thy womb, Jesus"?
300	Glory be to the Father, _____.	What comes before "and to the Son, and to the Holy Spirit"?
400	God from God, light from light, _____.	What comes before "true God from true God"?
500	I once was lost, _____.	What comes before "but now I'm found"?

THE BOAT

ON YOUR MARK!

- To empower young people to live out the Gospel more fully in everyday situations
- To enable leaders to get to know young people in the group

GET SET!

- Open the Bible to Matthew 14:23-33.
- If possible, have a small rowboat in your space. The reader could read from the boat.
- Post these signs around the room.

In the Boat	Trying to Step Out in Faith
Beginning to Sink	Reaching Out with a Saving Hand

GO!

- Have someone read aloud Matthew 14:23-33.
- As you read each of the following questions, ask young people to move to the sign that **best** describes how they feel. Once everyone has chosen a sign, invite teens to explain their choices.

1. Think of someone in your school who is hurting. In your relationship with this person, are you:
   - In the Boat (Are you afraid to reach out?)
   - Trying to Step Out in Faith (Are you beginning to commit to making a difference?)
   - Beginning to Sink (Are you losing faith because you are realizing what you got yourself into by trying to help?)
   - Reaching Out with a Saving Hand (Are you helping the person or getting others to help?)

2. Think of someone in your family who is going through a rough time. In your relationship with this person, are you:
   - In the Boat (Are you sitting tight?)
   - Trying to Step Out in Faith (Are you moving toward the person?)
   - Beginning to Sink (Are you in over your head?)
   - Reaching Out with a Saving Hand (Are you helping out or getting family and friends to help?)

3. The last time you were present when members of a group were picking on someone, were you:
   - In the Boat (Were you trying not to get involved?)
   - Trying to Step Out in Faith (Were you quietly saying a word or two to help the person out?)
   - Beginning to Sink (Were you trying to defend the person, but feeling like you were losing ground not only for the person, but also for yourself?)
   - Reaching Out with a Saving Hand (Were you feeling confident enough to speak out for the person, knowing you were in the right?)

4. Think of the last time you really hurt someone. In trying to reconcile with that person, were you:
   - In the Boat (Were you not wanting to get near the person?)
   - Trying to Step Out in Faith (Were you moving toward the person, but hesitantly, and not quite making it?)
   - Beginning to Sink (Were you so worried about how the conversation would go that you gave up and felt bad?)
   - Reaching Out with a Saving Hand (Knowing that it's not easy to reconcile, but that reconciliation is the right thing to do, you did your part.)

5. Think of an experience in your life that needs healing. In looking for support and healing, are you:
   - In the Boat (Are you avoiding looking for support and healing?)
   - Trying to Step Out in Faith (Are you making the first moves toward getting the help you need?)
   - Beginning to Sink (Are you feeling alone and not able to deal with the situation by yourself?)
   - Reaching Out with a Saving Hand (Are you talking to people you trust and actively looking for support and healing? Are you talking to God about the situation?)

6. In this group, do you feel you are:
   - In the Boat (You attend meetings, but don't risk much.)
   - Trying to Step Out in Faith (Are you willing to look at changing your life and sharing with others?)
   - Beginning to Sink (Are you feeling like you are investing a lot in the group, but not getting the support that you need?)
   - Reaching Out with a Saving Hand (Are you helping others to get out of the boat and offering them support when they need it? Are you looking for support from others and looking for the hand of Jesus to lift you, too?)

After they have considered all the questions, invite young people to come back together as a group and sit down. Ask them to reflect on the following questions and, if they are comfortable doing so, share what they are thinking.

When it comes to reconciliation, do you think you would be most likely to:

- Try to make peace?
- Hold a grudge?
- Try to get even?
- Try to ignore the situation that requires reconciliation?
- Did any of the questions you considered for this activity make you think about things in your life that you would like to think about or change? Why?

BAPTISM AT THE MOVIES

ON YOUR MARK!

- To present Baptism as a sacrament of initiation
- To help young people understand the significance of Baptism

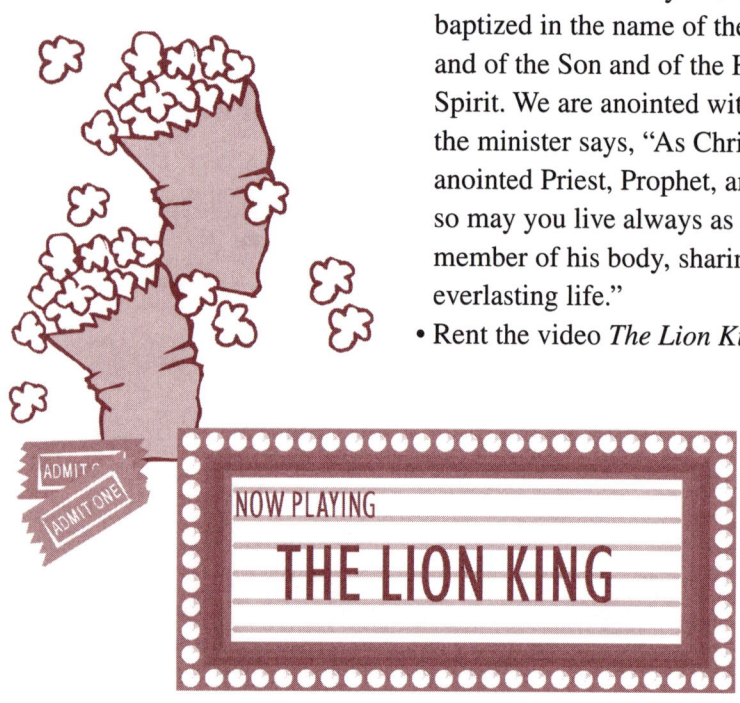

- To give young people the opportunity to meet either a couple whose child is going to be baptized or an adult who is about to be baptized

GET SET!

- Remind teens that there are three sacraments of initiation—Baptism, Confirmation, and Eucharist. In Baptism, we are initiated into the Christian community. We are baptized in the name of the Father and of the Son and of the Holy Spirit. We are anointed with oil as the minister says, "As Christ was anointed Priest, Prophet, and King, so may you live always as a member of his body, sharing everlasting life."
- Rent the video *The Lion King*.
- Ask the appropriate parish representative for the name of a couple whose child is about to be baptized or an adult who will be baptized at the Easter Vigil.
- Invite that couple or adult to speak to your group.

GO!

- Introduce your guest or guests.
- Show the scene near the beginning of *The Lion King* in which Simba is held up before the community. Ask these or similar questions.

  Why was Simba held up to the community?

  Do you think every new baby animal was presented this way?

  Or was this reserved for the offspring of leaders?

- Explain that in Baptism, we are presented to the community for initiation. Each of us is anointed with the words, "As Christ was anointed Priest, Prophet, and King, so may you live always as a member of his body, sharing everlasting life." Let teens know that in the kingdom of God, we are all royalty!
- Invite the parents to talk about their child's Baptism, including their hopes and dreams for their child, how and why they selected their child's name, and whatever other information they care to share.
- Invite the adult who is preparing for Baptism to explain why he or she wants to become a Catholic.
- Make plans for the young people to attend the Baptism.
- Ask young people to write notes welcoming the newly baptized to the Church. These can be presented at the Baptism.

SEPTEMBER DISCUSSION STARTER: THE RADIO STATION

ON YOUR MARK!

To help young people:
- See the need to make decisions based on moral principles
- Develop problem-solving skills
- Understand that people are more important than things

GET SET!

- Read the scenario yourself.
- Adapt the number of roles to the size of your group. If your group is large, ask young people to form two or more groups for this activity. If your group is small, reduce the number of roles.
- Have young people choose roles to take in the discussion of the scenario.
- Read, or have a volunteer read, the scenario aloud to the group.

GO!

SCENARIO

A local radio station has been rated number one in youth and young adult ratings. In fact, the station manager just received a sizable cash bonus because the ratings books show the station to be number one for the second consecutive year.

At about the same time, a police officer has been killed in your town. Found next to the officer's body was a CD. Among the selections on the CD is a song about "cop-killing," entitled "Run 'em Down, Gun 'em Down." The song has been played frequently on the radio station.

The radio station has also been playing songs that are racist and songs that are abusive to women. The local newspaper has called for the station to lose its license. Local groups are asking that the station manager be fired. Because he wants desperately to keep his job, the station manager has been trying to find ways to quiet the criticism. That would include promising not to play some of the music that the newspaper and other local groups find offensive. The station's most popular DJ, a shock jock who is number one in all the ratings books, has threatened to quit if the station manager gives in to pressure.

The town's young people are divided. Some are saying that violent lyrics have no effect on listeners. They argue that they listen to the station all the time, and they've never killed anyone. They aren't racist or abusive. Others are saying that violent lyrics do have an impact.

GATHERED AT THE DISCUSSION TABLE ARE:

- The station manager
- The shock jock
- Some supporters of the station
- Some who oppose the station
- The deceased police officer's spouse

Notes for Group Leaders

In the *Discussion Starter*, teens take on the roles of persons involved in this situation. They are "acting" in the initial discussion.

What is most important is to bring the discussion to a conclusion. After the discussion, ask young people to shift away from their roles and return to being themselves. Help teens to process the experience by asking questions such as these:

- What values are involved in this scenario?
- What Catholic teachings can be applied?
- How are those involved in this situation called to be Christ?

Young people deserve to be so much more than actors with roles: they are disciples of Christ, learning how to take faith to the marketplace!

YOUR TASK:

- Discuss the issue from the point of view of your role.
- As a group, decide what the station manager should do.

OCTOBER

OCTOBER-AT-A-GLANCE

Octopus, octave, October—all come from the Latin word *octo*, which means eight. This was the eighth month of the Roman calendar.

OCTOBER FROM A CATHOLIC CHRISTIAN PERSPECTIVE

October is in Ordinary Time. It is a beautiful month of seasonal changes—provided, of course, that one is fortunate enough to live in a place that has seasons. October is traditionally the month of the rosary, that great prayer of the Church. It is also the month of some really amazing saints! Let's hope it's an amazing month for those saints who are gathered with you!

GREAT CHURCH FEAST DAYS

2 **Guardian Angels**—This feast is dedicated to the pure spirits created by God to serve as God's messengers and to watch over human beings.

4 **St. Francis of Assisi** (d. 1226)—The founder of the Franciscan Order, St. Francis is credited with making popular the practice of setting up a crib as a memorial to Jesus' birth in a manger.

6 **St. Bruno** (d. 1101)—St. Bruno's devotion to prayer, reading, and manual work are practices still followed by the Carthusian Order, which he founded.

9 **St. Denis** (d. 258) **and Companions**—St. Denis, bishop of Paris, is regarded as the patron saint of France, despite the fact that he was beheaded there, along with other missionary bishops.

16 **St. Hedwig** (d. 1243)—In German, this saint's name means struggle. Her struggle was to help her husband and her children. Her faith and hope were honored by God with the gift of miracles.

18 **St. Luke** (first century)—Author of a gospel and the Acts of the Apostles, St. Luke traveled with St. Paul and was an eyewitness to many of St. Paul's miracles.

24 **St. Anthony Claret** (d. 1870)—St. Anthony is said to have preached 10,000 sermons and published 200 books and pamphlets. The Claretians, the order he founded, are still involved in publishing.

SAINT OF THE MONTH
St. Therese of Lisieux (1873-1897)

Therese Martin was born in 1873, the youngest of nine children, of which only five daughters lived. Her childhood was marked by her mother's death, when Therese was only four, her sisters' watchful care and tutoring, and her father's love. She struggled with her physical and emotional health and with the loss of all but one of her older sisters to religious life.

Faith was integral to the life of the Martin family. From an early age, Therese came to understand and experience her life—its gifts and challenges—through faith's lens. Everything—whether filled with pain or joy —was an opportunity to grow, to love, to pray, and to depend on God. Her love for God led her to become a Carmelite at fifteen. Therese's life continued in joy and in sorrow. Her father became seriously ill, both physically and mentally. Four of the Martin daughters eventually were together in the

CARVING OUT YOUR LIFE!

ON YOUR MARK!

- To enable young people to apply lessons from the ordinary to their own faith lives

GET SET!

- Prepare one large or several small pumpkins by cutting a lid out of the top of each pumpkin.

- Have available ice-cream scoops, carving tools, felt-tipped markers, lights for inside the pumpkins, and so on.

Carmel* at Lisieux. Therese, who directed the novices, wrote her autobiography under the direction of her sister Pauline, who was prioress. Therese died at twenty-four after an intensely painful illness.

Therese's greatest gift to the Church seems to be the example she gave for living an ordinary life with extraordinary awareness and grace. She wrote, "Love proves itself by deeds, so how am I to show my love? Great deeds are forbidden me. The only way I can prove my love is by scattering flowers and these flowers are every little sacrifice, every glance and word, and the doing of the least actions for love." She was big on random acts of kindness and on keeping them secret!

Thousands of Catholics identified with Therese's search for holiness through the ordinary. She was canonized in 1925, just twenty-seven years after her death, and is one of the patron saints of the missions because of her special love of the missions. At the 1997 celebration of World Youth Day in Paris, she was named a doctor of the Church, only the third woman to be so honored. Even though she thought of herself as a small and much loved child of God, she became a strong and faith-filled force in her Carmel,* and in her world. She is remembered on her feast day, October 3.

Carmel is the name Carmelites give to their monasteries and convents in honor of Mount Carmel, in the Holy Land, where their order was founded.

GO!

- Explain that pumpkins can tell us a lot about ourselves! Just as we carve pumpkins, God has carved, or designed, us. After each stage of carving, we will reflect on God's word and learn about ourselves.

- Ask young people to use ice-cream scoops to clean out all of the G.P.G. (Genuine Pumpkin Gunk).
- Read, or have a volunteer read:

God takes the time to purify us and help us get rid of all that will rot or decay. As it says in the book of Ezekiel,

> I will sprinkle clean water upon you, and you shall be clean from all your uncleannesses, and from all your idols I will cleanse you. A new heart I will give you, and a new spirit I will put within you; and I will remove from your body the heart of stone and give you a heart of flesh. I will put my spirit within you, and make you follow my statutes and be careful to observe my ordinances.
>
> Ezekiel 36:25-27

- Have teens draw a friendly face onto each pumpkin.
- Read, or have a volunteer read:

God has created each of us in a unique and wonderful way. Yet, we have one thing in common: each of us is made, or carved out, in the image and likeness of God. For Scripture says:

> So God created humankind in his image,
> in the image of God he created them;
> male and female he created them.
>
> Genesis 1:27

- Carve, or have a volunteer or volunteers carve, the eyes.
- Read, or have a volunteer read:

Each of us has our eyes opened in so many different ways. Our eyes help us to see and appreciate the world. As the psalmist says,

> Open my eyes, so that I may behold
>   wondrous things out of your law.
>
> Psalm 119:18

That is a prayer for each of us, that we could see God's wonders more clearly.

- Carve, or have a volunteer or volunteers carve, the nose.
- Read, or have a volunteer read:

They say that one of our strongest senses is the sense of smell. That we can remember smells longer than what we hear or touch is amazing. Our sense of smell lets us take in the sweet smell of an apple pie baking or warns us of fire in the area. Our sense of smell is something that we take for granted. But it allows us to breathe in the very goodness of God. Scripture tells us:

> If the whole body were an eye, where would the hearing be? If the whole body were hearing, where would the sense of smell be? But as it is, God arranged the members in the body, each one of them, as he chose.
>
> 1 Corinthians 12:17-18

- Carve, or have a volunteer or volunteers carve, the mouth.
- Read, or have a volunteer read:

Our mouths can get us into lots of trouble. But they also can be used to say a word of encouragement or express a wish of peace. Scripture tells us that our mouths are directly tied to our hearts. Matthew 12:34 says:

> For out of the abundance of the heart the mouth speaks.

If we keep our hearts focused on good, we will talk about good.

- Add a light to the pumpkin or pumpkins.
- Read, or have a volunteer read:

> You are the light of the world. A city built on a hill cannot be hid. No one after lighting a lamp puts it under the bushel basket, but on the lampstand, and it gives light to all in the house. In the same way, let your light shine before others, so that they may see your good works and give glory to your Father in heaven.
>
> Matthew 5:14-16

> Who is like the wise [person]?
> And who knows the interpretation of a thing?
> Wisdom makes one's face shine,
>   and the hardness of one's countenance is changed.
>
> Ecclesiastes 8:1

We must be the light of the world! We must be wise people! We must let the light of Christ shine through us. Pumpkins can tell us a lot about ourselves!

HOME SWEET HOME

ON YOUR MARK!
- To help young people examine the ways in which we can build our lives

GET SET!
- Build a house out of Legos®.
- Make sure there are enough Legos in the house so that each young person can have one.
- Provide felt-tipped pens for young people to share.

GO!
- Read this story aloud to the young people.

There's a story I've heard,
It has been around for years.
If you listen to its moral,
It could save you many tears.

The story is about a craftsman
Who was regarded around town
To do some of the finest carpentry
That could ever be found.

It was really quite amazing,
His quality and his skill,
The beauty of his craft,
His determination and will.

His heart's greatest desire
Was to do each job with care
So when he finished a new house,
A family would be proud to live there.

Well, the craftsman finally wearied.
He would too easily tire,
And he wanted just to enjoy life.
Building was no longer his desire.

So he went to the owner
And said he wanted to retire,
Said that he was finished building,
Said he had lost his heart's fire.

The owner looked into his eyes,
And then he raised his glass,
"We will miss you, my dear friend.
Go ahead! Make this project your last."

So the builder finished his last work,
Perhaps the greatest work of this man,
And he went to see his boss to retire
According to the plan.

The owner met the craftsman,
And said, "I cannot let you go.
I've read your contract, you've six months left.
You must be disappointed, I know.

"But there's a house that I need built.
It is for a special friend.
I'm afraid I'm going to enforce the contract,
Your work has yet to end."

The craftsman got up and left the room.
Not a single word was said.
Anger welled up within him,
He wished the owner dead.

"For years I've worked for that old man,
And I've worked hard and long.
For him to treat me like this,
It is unfair, unjust, and wrong."

And so off he went to his new site.
Drowning in misery
He resolved that he would "fix" the owner,
And get even. He would see!

He went to work on the house
Using shoddy equipment.
He alone would guarantee
The money would be poorly spent.

He used nails that were too short,
And boards that were warped and stressed.
He gave too little time for the walls to dry.
Instead of measuring, he'd just guess.

The last work was his poorest effort.
He did his weakest work.
When it was over, he saw the boss.
"Your house is finished," he said with a smirk.

"Thank you," said the boss.
"Now you may retire, as you please,
But…one more thing," the owner said,
"Here are your new keys."

The craftsman looked shocked, don't you know!
Imagine his surprise.
The owner had given him the house,
And tears filled his eyes.

He thought about the work he did,
Knowing he would now live there,
And said to himself, "Had I known that,
I would have taken better care."

Each of us has a house to build,
A house where we reside.
The house we build is called our life.
Poor work is hard to hide.

So remember the story of the builder,
And build with the best in your life.
Measure always, choose carefully,
And avoid the builder's strife!

- Ask young people to reflect on the "houses" they've built. To begin, invite each young person to take one piece from the Lego house.
- Ask them to write on one side of their Legos one thing they would really like to do before they are thirty.
- Ask them to write on another side what one characteristic they would like to be foundational in their lives.
- Ask them to write on another side what characteristic they admire most in a person whom they regard highly.
- Ask them to write on the fourth side a gift God has given them that they do not want to squander in the building of their lives.

CONFIRMATION AT THE MOVIES

ON YOUR MARK!
- To provide a springboard for a discussion of Confirmation

GET SET!
- Rent the video *Armageddon*.
- Preview the movie.

GO!
- Introduce the movie by briefly summarizing the plot. An asteroid described as being the size of Texas is heading toward earth. Unless something can be done, the impact will destroy the earth. NASA has eighteen days to come up with a solution. NASA officials hire Harry Stamper and his gang of oilmen to save the planet by drilling through the asteroid. In the scene you are about to show, it is determined that a nuclear device will need to be detonated. Whoever detonates the device will be killed.
- Show the scene that begins with the statement, "Gruber is dead." Stop the video after Harry's conversation with his daughter.
- Discuss Harry's offer to die so that others can live.

   Why is he so willing to sacrifice his life?

   What do you think motivates someone who is willing to make a sacrifice for others?

   Who really died to save the world?

   How does the sacrifice of Jesus challenge us to live our lives?

   In Confirmation, which is one of the three sacraments of initiation, we are given gifts for the service of the community. What gifts did you see exhibited in the movie?

OCTOBER DISCUSSION STARTER: THE CONVENIENCE STORE

ON YOUR MARK!

To help young people:
- See the need to make decisions based on moral principles
- Develop problem-solving skills
- Understand that people are more important than things

GET SET!

- Read the scenario yourself.
- Adapt the number of roles to the size of your group. If your group is large, ask young people to form two or more groups for this activity. If your group is small, reduce the number of roles.
- Have young people choose roles to take in a discussion of the scenario.
- Read, or have a volunteer read, the scenario aloud to the group.

GO!

SCENARIO

The local convenience store has been the victim of teenage shoplifters. They have been coming into the store in groups of five or more, creating diversions, and then shoplifting. This has caused significant losses in the store. The storeowner has implemented two new policies. First is that only one teen is allowed in the store at a time. Second is that the storeowner will blast classical music outside the store so that young people do not congregate there. Local youth have been riding by, shouting obscenities at the store, and throwing eggs. The storeowner has made it clear that he will shoot anyone who threatens his security or the security of his employees. Tempers are flaring.

GATHERED AT THE DISCUSSION TABLE ARE:

- A representative from the police department
- The storeowner
- Local youth
- A couple of the alleged shoplifters
- A youth minister

YOUR TASK:

- Discuss the issue from the point of view of your role.
- As a group, try to come up with a resolution for the conflict.
- If the conflict has been resolved, create a slogan that reflects that resolution. If the group has not been able to resolve the conflict, create slogans that reflect the different positions.

Notes for Group Leaders

In the *Discussion Starter*, teens take on roles of those involved in this situation. They are "acting" in the initial discussion.

What is most important is to bring the discussion to a conclusion. After the discussion, ask young people to shift away from their roles and return to being themselves. Help teens to process the experience by asking questions such as these:

- What values are involved in this scenario?
- What Catholic teachings can be applied?
- How are those involved in this situation called to be Christ?

Young people deserve to be so much more than actors with roles: they are disciples of Christ, learning how to take faith to the marketplace!

NOVEMBER

NOVEMBER-AT-A-GLANCE

November comes from the Latin word *novem*, meaning nine. November was the ninth month of the early Roman calendar.

NOVEMBER FROM A CATHOLIC CHRISTIAN PERSPECTIVE

What a great month November is in the Church! We celebrate saints and souls. We celebrate the communion of saints—all those who have come before, all those who are, all those who will be. We celebrate those souls who have touched our lives—all those who have "gone before us marked with the sign of faith" (Eucharistic Prayer 1), for whom life has changed, not ended. What a great month November is!

GREAT CHURCH FEAST DAYS

1 All Saints Day—On this day the Church celebrates not only saints, but all who have lived lives of faith.

2 All Souls Day—Masses are offered for all the faithful departed.

11 St. Martin of Tours (d. 387)—The story is told that when St. Martin was a soldier, he once cut his own cloak in half so that he could share it with a beggar. St. Martin left the army to spread the word of Christ.

16 St. Gertrude the Great (d. 1302)—St. Gertrude is known for her devotion to the Sacred Heart of Jesus and for her inspirational writings.

17 St. Rose Philippine Duchesne (d. 1852)—Born in Grenoble, France, St. Rose Philippine Duchesne became a missionary on the American frontier.

30 St. Andrew (first century)—Present at the baptism of Jesus, St. Andrew became a follower of Jesus and brought his brother, Peter, to meet Jesus.

SAINT OF THE MONTH
St. Martin de Porres (1579-1639)

Martin de Porres was born in Lima, Peru, in 1579, to a biracial couple. He was the child of a black former slave from Panama and a Spanish knight. As a teen, he joined the Dominicans in Lima and became a lay brother. His work was not flashy. His life was grounded in the ordinary. He is reported to have worked on a farm, in the laundry and kitchen. He nursed the sick and gave alms with great love to the poor. As he lived his faith in ordinary ways, he also consulted with the leadership of his order and with bishops, was a close friend of St. Rose of Lima, and was known for his great love for all God's creation and his devotion to spiritual disciplines. His own birth linked him with minorities, and he reached out to all, with particular care for slaves brought in from Africa. St. Martin de Porres is the patron saint of interracial justice and harmony. His feast day is November 3.

REMEMBRANCE QUILT*

ON YOUR MARK!

- To deepen young people's awareness of the communion of saints
- To provide an opportunity for young people to pray for those who have gone before us in faith

GET SET!

- You will need to enlist the help of a quilter from your parish. Provide that person with a copy of these instructions.
- Check with the quilter about what materials he or she may need.
- A week before this activity, ask young people to bring in at least two twelve-inch squares of a solid-color cotton material. One will be decorated for the top of the quilt. The other will be used for the backing of the decorated square.
- Have them also find the names and check on the stories of family members or family friends who have died.
- Provide materials to be used in decorating the cloth squares: magazines, glue sticks, markers, colored pencils, yarn, scraps of material, scissors.
- Optional: Obtain computer iron-on t-shirt transfers for teens to use in decorating their squares.

GO!

- Talk with the young people about All Saints Day and All Souls Day. Let them know that November has become a very special month of remembrance.
- If possible, introduce young people to the quilter who will assist on this project.
- Tell young people to decorate one of their squares with a person's name, telling the person's story in words or in art. They can glue on pictures if they like.
- When everyone has decorated a square (or two or three depending on the size of your group), ask the young people to take turns telling a little about their squares. If it is possible for the quilter to be present, ask the quilter to collect the squares. If not, collect the squares and get them to the quilter. Pin each teen's squares together.
- The quilter then sews the squares into a quilt.
- The group has just made a Remembrance Quilt that can be used to decorate your prayer space for the month of November.

*This activity could easily be expanded and done as a parish activity.

WHO WANTS TO BE A CATHOLIC MILLIONAIRE?

ON YOUR MARK!
- To allow young people to have fun while exploring what it means to be Catholic

GET SET!
- Buy ten $100,000 candy bars to make a million-dollar prize.
- Buy small candies for rewards for correct answers to questions with lesser values.
- If possible, dress like Regis Fill-In.

GO!
- Play background music that the young people will enjoy.
- Divide the group into teams. Depending on the size of your group, a team can consist of one to seven members.
- Explain that teens will work as teams for all of the questions except the last one. The group that is ahead before the last round chooses a team representative. That representative needs to answer the last question correctly to get the million dollars' worth of candy for his or her team. If no one answers correctly, you can distribute the million dollars of candy in any way that's fair. Correct answers are in red.

Question Number One, for $100
Which of the following is NOT one of the seven sacraments?
a. Baptism
b. Holy Orders
c. Penance
d. Monday-night football

Question Number Two, for $200
Which of the following is not a sacrament of initiation?
a. Baptism
b. Confirmation
c. Eucharist
d. Eagle Scout

Question Number Three, for $300
The writers of the Gospels are:
a. John, Paul, George, and Ringo
b. John, Paul, Peter, and James
c. Mark, Matthew, Luke, and John
d. Abraham, Martin, and John

Question Number Four, for $500
Character sacraments are sacraments that the Church does not repeat. Which of the following is NOT a character sacrament?
a. Baptism
b. Eucharist
c. Confirmation
d. Holy Orders

Question Number Five, for $1,000
Mass comes from the term meaning:
a. A large gathering
b. A growth
c. Dismissal
d. Communion

Question Number Six, for $2,000
Absolution is part of this sacrament, which has been referred to as all of the following except:
a. Concentration
b. Confession
c. Reconciliation
d. Penance

Question Number Seven, for $4,000
RCIA stands for:
a. Rich Catholics in America
b. Roman Catholic Intelligence Agency
c. Rite of Christian Initiation of Adults
d. Roman Catholicism In Action

Question Number Eight, for $8,000
This special night is the greatest feast of the Church year:
a. Midnight Mass
b. Easter Vigil
c. Pentecost Sunday
d. Good Friday

Question Number Nine, for $16,000
In Holy Orders, one can be ordained a:
a. Deacon, priest, and bishop
b. Priest, monsignor, and bishop
c. Deacon, priest, bishop, and pope
d. Priest, bishop, archbishop, and pope

Question Number Ten, for $32,000
The word *Gospel* means:
a. Thanksgiving
b. Good news
c. God's love
d. Great music

Question Number Eleven, for $64,000
The pope is known by all of these titles but one:
a. Holy Father
b. Successor of Noah
c. Bishop of Rome
d. Vicar of Christ

Question Number Twelve, for $125,000
Often, a pope takes the name of a predecessor. So Pope John Paul II took the name of John Paul I. Which of the following names does not have a successor as pope?
a. Paul
b. Pius
c. Peter
d. John

Question Number Thirteen, for $250,000
Epistle is:
a. Latin for Gospels
b. Greek for Gospels
c. A letter
d. A question

Question Number Fourteen, for $500,000
The correct liturgical color for Ordinary Time is:
a. Green
b. Blue
c. Red
d. White

Question Number Fifteen, for $1,000,000
In the Scriptures, Luke was said to have a certain profession. Luke was a:
a. Tax collector
b. Actor
c. Physician
d. Lawyer

Bonus or Substitute Question
Who painted the ceiling of the Sistine Chapel?
a. Michelangelo
b. Donatello
c. Raphael
d. Leonardo

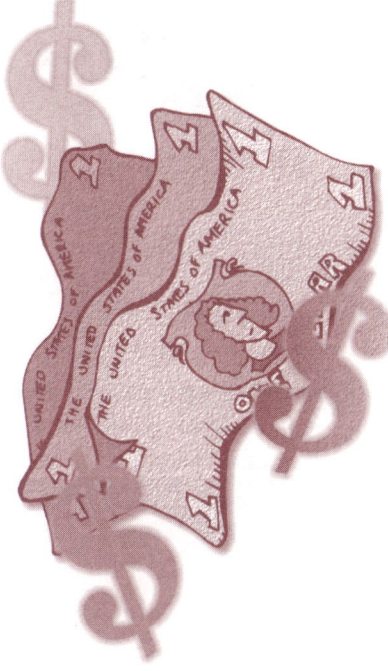

EUCHARIST AT THE MOVIES

ON YOUR MARK!
- To provide a springboard for a discussion of Eucharist

GET SET!
- Rent the movie *Phenomenon*.
- Preview the movie.

NOW PLAYING
PHENOMENON

GO!
- Introduce the movie by briefly summarizing the plot. A phenomenon in the nighttime sky is believed to have transformed a rural mechanic into a genius with psychic powers. The mechanic is in love with a mother of two children. It turns out the mechanic has a brain tumor and is about to die. Toward the end of the movie, the mechanic and the two children are working on a car. One of the children asks the mechanic about his impending death. Begin to show the movie at this point. End after the apple scene.
- Ask what the mechanic taught the children about the apple. Remind them how the mechanic identified with the apple while dining with those he loved.
- Remind teens that Jesus took bread and wine. He, too, said there was something important about this. Jesus said to his friends, "This is my body" and "This is my blood." In the movie the apple became part of all three of the characters. In the gift of the Eucharist, the bread and wine become the body and blood of Jesus Christ. And when we receive the Eucharist, we are changed forever!

NOVEMBER DISCUSSION STARTER: THE MEDICAL TEST

ON YOUR MARK!
To help young people:
- See the need to make decisions based on moral principles
- Develop problem-solving skills
- Understand that people are more important than things

GET SET!
- Read the scenario yourself.
- Adapt the number of roles to the size of your group. If your group is large, ask young people to form two or more groups for this activity. If your group is small, reduce the number of roles.
- Have young people select roles to take in a discussion of the scenario.
- Read, or have a volunteer read, the scenario aloud to the group.

GO!

SCENARIO
Mary and Rick, who have known one another since high school, are engaged to be married in three months. In their mid-twenties, both are finishing up medical school and are ready to start their lives together.

Rick has always felt that his life began the day he met Mary. He already feels as if he is part of Mary's family. Because his own dad died when he was only four, Mary's dad is the only father Rick ever knew. But Rick always considered his mom amazing. She made sure Rick always knew how much he was loved.

To get all of the necessary paperwork ready for their marriage, Mary and Rick go to the city records department to get a certified copy of Rick's birth certificate. On a whim, Rick asks for a copy of his dad's death certificate.

When he reads the certificate, something stops him cold. After a profound moment of silence, he looks at Mary and says, "I was always told that Dad died from complications of a war injury. This says that Dad died from Akeroid's disease. Mom never really talked about Dad's death to me, and I never pressed her. She would just sob. Now I know why."

Mary knows why, too. Akeroid's is a genetic disease that is passed on to one out of every two children. Symptoms usually appear between the ages of thirty and fifty, sometimes even earlier. This progressive disease causes its victims to experience personality changes and a loss of mental functions. People with Akeroid's often lose their ability to calculate or make judgments. They can even lose their ability to speak. Their bodies often make quick, jerky uncontrollable movements. There is no cure, and the disease usually kills its victims within fifteen to twenty years.

Rick and Mary both cry. They hope that maybe—just maybe—the death certificate is wrong. But as soon as they tell Rick's mother that they have the certificate, they know the truth. Rick's mom cries, too.

They know that a test is available to tell Rick whether or not he will get the disease. If he takes the test and it is positive, Rick feels that the next ten years of his life would be hell, with a kind of death sentence hanging over his head. If he doesn't take the test, he and Mary won't know what to expect.

Rick wants to call off the wedding. He wants to live the next ten years fully. Ten years, and maybe more. He feels that he can be guaranteed at least ten years to start his medical practice and live out his dream. But he does not feel he should ask Mary to live with uncertainty.

Mary wants Rick to have the test. She tells him she will marry him whether or not he will get the disease, but she wants to know. She doesn't want that gene to be passed on to her children.

Mary's family wants her to leave Rick if he won't have the test. They consider it God's providence that Mary and Rick have discovered this potential problem before the wedding. They love Rick, but they feel that marriage is out of the question if the two can't know what their future might bring.

GATHERED AROUND THE DISCUSSION TABLE ARE:
- Rick
- Rick's mother
- Mary
- Mary's Dad
- Friends who think Mary and Rick should go ahead with their marriage
- Friends who think the two should not marry
- The priest who is supposed to marry them

YOUR TASK:
- Talk to Rick openly and honestly from the point of view of your role.

Notes for Group Leaders

In the *Discussion Starter*, teens are encouraged to take on roles of those involved in this situation. They are "acting" in the initial discussion.

What is most important is to bring the discussion to a conclusion. After the discussion, ask young people to shift away from their roles and return to being themselves. Help teens to process the experience by asking questions such as these:

- What values are involved in this scenario?
- What Catholic teachings can be applied?
- How are those involved in this situation called to be Christ?

Young people deserve to be so much more than actors with roles: they are disciples of Christ, learning how to take faith into their lives!

DECEMBER

DECEMBER-AT-A-GLANCE

December comes from the Latin word *decem,* meaning ten; it was the tenth month on the Roman Calendar.

DECEMBER FROM A CATHOLIC CHRISTIAN PERSPECTIVE

Ask any child what December means from a Catholic Christian perspective!

🎀 GREAT CHURCH FEAST DAYS

6   St. Nicholas (fourth century)—Stories about St. Nicholas's acts of charity have led to his being considered the patron of children and the saintly model for Santa Claus.

8   Immaculate Conception of the Blessed Virgin Mary—On this feast we celebrate a truth of our faith—that Mary was conceived and born free from all stain of sin.

13 St. Lucy (d. 304)—Possibly because her name means light, St. Lucy is the patron of the blind and all who suffer from eye trouble.

21 St. Peter Canisius (d. 1597)—This energetic and tireless Jesuit theologian wrote two very popular catechisms and is honored as the founder of the Catholic press.

25 Nativity of the Lord, Christmas!

26 St. Stephen (first century)—One of the first deacons of the Church, St. Stephen was stoned for preaching the good news of Jesus. Saul, who would later become the apostle Paul, was among those who watched.

27 St. John the Evangelist (first century)—St. John, the only apostle to stand at the foot of the cross, was asked by Jesus to care for Mary.

29 St. Thomas Becket (d. 1170)—St. Thomas Becket, the Archbishop of Canterbury, was martyred defending the rights of the Church against the aggressive king of England.

30 The Feast of the Holy Family—Jesus, Mary, and Joseph are honored on the Sunday that falls within the octave of Christmas. If no Sunday falls within these eight days, the feast is celebrated on December 30.

SAINT OF THE MONTH
Our Lady of Guadalupe

When Mary appeared to native Mexican Juan Diego in 1531, she was dressed as a beautiful Aztec princess and spoke to him in the Aztec language. The appearances of Mary and her special gifts of roses, a healing, and her image on Juan's mantle—all touched hearts where the missionaries who first came to Mexico with the conquistadors had been unsuccessful. Mary's approach to the Mexicans as Our Lady of Guadalupe celebrated their culture and pointed to her Son, Jesus. Christianity's first face in Mexico could be said to have been Mary's.

Our Lady of Guadalupe is the patron of the Americas. Recently Pope John Paul II challenged the Church in America to see itself as united. (See *Ecclesia in America*.)

BLESSED ARE THE PEACEMAKERS AND THE PIECEMAKERS!

ON YOUR MARK!

- To help young people to learn about peacemakers and leaders in justice and service
- To create an opportunity for young people to be teachers of children

Our Lady of Guadalupe teaches all to find and celebrate her Son in and through the richness of every culture. Her feast day is celebrated on December 12.

GET SET!

For this activity, you will need:
- Posters of Dr. Martin Luther King, Jr., Dorothy Day, Rosa Parks, Mother Teresa, Archbishop Romero, and others associated with justice and service. (You will need one poster for each young person.)
- Styrofoam artboard on which to mount the posters. (The sheets of artboard could be larger than the posters and could be cut to size later.)
- A utility knife for each adult who will be cutting puzzle pieces
- Felt-tipped pens to be shared and a pencil for each participant
- To arrange to visit an elementary school group, or to arrange for an elementary school group to visit your site

GO!

FIRST SESSION

- Display the posters.
- Ask young people to talk about the stories of the peacemakers pictured on the posters. Be prepared to fill in details as necessary.
- Encourage young people to discuss which of the peacemakers inspire them and why.
- Explain that the young people are going to be piecemakers. They will create jigsaw puzzles. These can be either classic puzzles in which pieces interlock or puzzles in which the pieces just come together nicely in rounded contours. Young people will share their puzzles with a group of elementary school children to celebrate Dr. King's birthday, which will be observed in January.
- Give each young person a poster. Help young people fasten their posters to the artboard by using an acid-free spray adhesive on the backs of the posters and then laying them gently on the artboard. Teens will need to make sure that their posters are flat and smooth by working out air pockets and wrinkles. Give young people time to make sure that their posters have no wrinkles, bumps, air pockets, or other imperfections that could cause problems later in the process!
- Have young people lay the sheets of artboard image side down on a

flat surface, weighing the sheets down evenly with books. Because these posters will take hours to dry, this will be all you can do in this first session.
- Explain that young people will need to do some homework to prepare for their meeting with the children. First, challenge each young person to watch a video about a peacemaker. Suggest some good movies about Dr. King, the civil rights movement, Dorothy Day, Mother Teresa, and others. Also challenge young people to read about the peacemaker who inspires them and to read Dr. King's sermons or his "I have a dream" speech. They may want to search for this information on internet sites.
- If possible, have a guest speaker talk to young people about what segregation was like.

SECOND SESSION

- Use a utility knife or scissors to cut the artboard to the shapes that young people want. If, for instance, a young person wanted his or her poster to feature only Dr. King's head and shoulders, cut the poster to that image. If young people want their posters to stay intact, cut rectangles by tracing the borders of the poster.
- Ask young people to turn the artboard facedown and trace the pieces for their puzzles. Remind them to make each piece large enough so that young children will be able to put the puzzles together. Ask teens to keep in mind the puzzles they put together when they were children!

Young people can use pencils to draw shapes for the puzzle pieces. Advise them to start with one corner and work along the edges to the next corner. They can rotate their posters, working from corner to corner. Once they have worked along the edges, they move inward and work the same way until they reach the center. Then ask them to evaluate their work by looking at all the pieces. Are any too small? Are any too thin? If so, they can erase and redraw. When they are satisfied, they can darken and broaden the pencil lines with a felt-tipped pen.

Ask them to label each puzzle piece, working the same way that they did to shape the pieces, starting with the outside and working to the center. Since small children can sometimes mix puzzle pieces together, labeling will help to keep the pieces for each puzzle together. For a Martin Luther King puzzle, pieces can be labeled MLK 1, MLK 2, MLK 3, and so on.
- Once puzzles are completed, cut the lines with a fine-tipped utility knife. The pieces should be cut in the same manner that they were drawn, that is, starting at the outside, going from corner to corner, and ending at the center. As you cut each piece, hand it to the puzzle-maker, who can put all the pieces together and check over the finished product. Invite other adults to help you with this step.
- Have each young person prepare and be ready to present a brief story that will tell children something about the person on his or her poster.
- When the group gathers with elementary school children, ask young people to tell the stories of the people on their posters. When all the stories have been told, have each young person work with a small group of children to put the puzzle together. Remind them as they work that they have just become piecemakers and peacemakers!

WITNESS!

ON YOUR MARK!

- To enable young people to prepare answers for this question: If someone accused you of being a Christian, would there be enough evidence to convict you?
- To help them to look at what it means to be Catholic

GET SET!

- Provide copies of **Handout 1: Witness Questions**, one for each person in the group.

GO!

- Read the account on this page, inviting all participants to pretend that they are meeting Chris's grandfather for the first time.
- Ask young people to form Group One and Group Two, with half assigned to each group. Then have individuals pair off so that there is a Number One and a Number Two in each pair. Assign Questions 1-7 to the Number Ones and Questions 8-14 to the Number Twos. Have teens ask and respond to the questions for individuals in these pairs.
- The facilitator can choose to take the role of Chris's grandfather to direct all the actions for the group, being sure that all participate. Or young people can take turns directing the actions.

You have fallen totally, completely, and unequivocally in love with Chris. And Chris with you! You decide to marry, and you plan your wedding date for this time next year. You have met almost everyone in Chris's family, and they seem to think that you are great. But they have all jokingly warned you that you don't get to marry Chris until you've met Chris's grandfather.

You know that Pop-Pop played a big role in Chris's growing up. You've heard Pop-Pop stories for almost as long as you have known Chris. You are nervous about meeting him.

Finally the day arrives for you to meet Chris's Pop-Pop. He welcomes you into his house. He gives you a soft drink and speaks to you about the good old days. His stories are great, his laughter infectious. You're wondering why everyone warned you about him. Then you find out.

Pop-Pop says, "Enough of this small talk. Tell me about yourself." So you tell him that you are the most accomplished person in your family, that you have a good job, a steady income, and that you are Catholic. To the last statement, Chris's grandfather says, "Prove it."

"Prove what, sir?" you ask.

And he repeats, "Prove to me you are Catholic."

You feel panic set in. You struggle for an answer. Then Pop-Pop begins throwing questions at you. You know you must answer correctly and completely.

Handout 1 &a Witness Questions

QUESTIONS FOR INDIVIDUALS

1. What is the name of the pastor of your parish?

2. What other staff members can you name?

3. What Church groups do you participate in? What do you like about these groups?

4. Who are the four Gospel writers?

5. What are the seven sacraments?

6. Name the three persons of the Trinity.

7. The four marks of the Church are that it is one, holy, catholic, and what?

8. What do you remember about your First Communion?

9. Who is your favorite saint? Why?

10. What is your favorite Scripture story? Why?

11. What is a prayer you use in tough times?

12. Name a person in the Church who has influenced your life. This person can be someone you either know or have read about.

13. What object in your house indicates that you are Catholic?

14. What is the most beautiful or striking or different church you've ever been in? Describe it.

ACTIONS FOR THE GROUP

1. Genuflect together.

2. Sing one verse of a common song or hymn.

3. Pantomime your parish's outreach for those who are in need.

RECONCILIATION AT THE MOVIES

ON YOUR MARK!

- To provide a springboard for a discussion of the sacrament of Reconciliation

GET SET!

- Rent the movie *Les Miserables*.
- Preview the beginning of the movie, including the scene that ends with the bishop giving Valjean the candlesticks and talking with him.

GO!

- Show that scene of the movie.
- Ask these or similar questions.

  What turned Valjean into such a hardened criminal?

  What turned the bishop into such a good man?

  What motivated the bishop to forgiveness?

  Describe an instance in which you have seen a person transformed by an act of kindness or forgiveness?

  What does this scene have to do with reconciliation? With the sacrament of Reconciliation?

DECEMBER DISCUSSION STARTER: THE PARISH GIFT

ON YOUR MARK!

To help young people:
- See the need to make decisions based on moral principles
- Develop problem-solving skills
- Understand that people are more important than things

GET SET!

- Read the scenario yourself.
- Adapt the number of roles to the size of your group. If your group is large, ask young people to form two or more groups for this activity. If your group is small, reduce the number of roles.
- Have young people choose roles to take in a discussion of the scenario.
- Provide copies of **Handout 2: Wish List**, one for each participant.
- Read, or have a volunteer read, the scenario aloud to the group.

GO!

SCENARIO

Your parish has been given $50,000 by a very generous parishioner. The money must be spent during the current fiscal year. The donor's only request is that the parish use the money in such a way that it reflects Gospel priorities. The people of the parish have been asked how they would like the money spent. They have come up with a long "wish list." You are responsible for distributing the money and explaining what Gospel priority is being reflected.

SEATED AT THE DISCUSSION TABLE ARE:

- The pastor
- A member of the parish council who has to vote on priorities
- A member of the school staff
- A member of the youth ministry team
- A member of social justice committee
- Several parishioners who want to do the best for everyone

YOUR TASK:

- Come up with a plan to use the money. Remember, you cannot put it into savings. This money must be used this year.
- Then decide whether the spending plan reflects Gospel values.
- If necessary, make changes in the plan to reflect Gospel values.

Notes for Group Leaders

In the *Discussion Starter*, teens take on roles of persons involved in this situation. They are "acting" in the initial discussion.

What is most important is to bring the discussion to a conclusion. After the discussion, ask young people to shift away from their roles and return to being themselves. Help teens to process the experience by asking questions such as these:

- What values are involved in this scenario?
- What Catholic teachings can be applied?
- How are those involved in this situation called to be Christ?

Young people deserve to be so much more than actors with roles: they are disciples of Christ, learning how to take faith into their community!

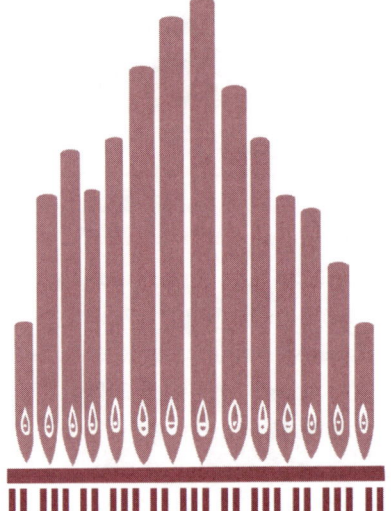

Handout 2 — Wish List

- **Youth ministry**
  $18,500 to purchase a van and $3,000 to fund a Habitat for Humanity project

- **Religious education**
  $22,500 to fund a new special education program

- **Seniors**
  $5,000 to provide hot lunches for the elderly

- **The prayer group**
  $36,000 to build a eucharistic chapel for prayer and private devotion

- **The committee responsible for the nursery**
  $4,000 to pay someone to coordinate the nursery during Masses

- **The parish secretary**
  $4,000 to purchase a new copier

- **The social justice committee**
  $5,000, or ten percent of the donation, to go to the poor

- **The pastor**
  $18,000 to repair the leak in the rectory roof

- **The school principal**
  $20,000 for tuition aid for families who need help

- **The contemporary music group**
  $6,000 for new hymnals

- **Elderly and handicapped parishioners**
  $32,500 to make the parish buildings more accessible

- **The pastoral associate**
  $2,200 for camera and sound and lighting equipment to videotape Masses for parish shut-ins, and $750 for a video series for Baptism preparation for new parents

- **The Confirmation coordinator**
  $500 to replace the Confirmation banners

- **The men's club**
  $3,000 to install and maintain a satellite dish to improve TV reception

- **The liturgy committee**
  $25,000 to fund an evangelization revival featuring Christian rock artists and dynamic preachers

- **The groundskeeper**
  $450 to repair a lawn tractor

- **The church organist**
  $17,500 to repair the organ

- **The building and grounds committee**
  $50,000 to repair the parking lot

JANUARY

JANUARY-AT-A-GLANCE

January is named for the Roman god Janus, whose two faces looked in opposite directions. He was the god of doorways and gateways, the god of entrances and beginnings. The month that opens the new year was named to honor Janus.

JANUARY FROM A CATHOLIC CHRISTIAN PERSPECTIVE

We worship the true God of new beginnings! Grounded in our faith, we open wide the doors to Christ Jesus! But we, too, look back and forward. Our liturgical calendar celebrates the Feast of the Holy Family on the Sunday after Christmas, and then we begin the year with the Solemnity of Mary the Mother of God on January 1. Because these two feasts highlight the significance of family to Christ Jesus and because this time of year brings us close to our families, family activities are the focus for January.

GREAT CHURCH FEAST DAYS

1 **The Solemnity of Mary, the Mother of God**—This is the oldest of the feasts on which the Church honors Mary throughout the year.

4 **St. Elizabeth Ann Seton** (d. 1821)—A convert to Catholicism, St. Elizabeth Ann Seton became the first American-born saint.

5 **St. John Neumann** (d. 1860)—St. John Neumann was the first American bishop to be canonized.

6 **Epiphany of the Lord**—*Epiphany* comes from a Greek word that means manifestation, to show plainly. On this feast we commemorate the manifestation of God, through Christ, to the whole world, which is symbolized by the three wise men.

21 **St. Agnes** (d. 304)—St. Agnes was persecuted and eventually martyred when, as a very young girl, she consecrated her virginity to God.

25 **The Conversion of St. Paul** (first century)—Saul persecuted Christians until his conversion. Then, as Paul, he preached that Christianity is the faith for all of humanity and became known as the apostle to the Gentiles.

29 **St. Francis de Sales** (d. 1622)—St. Francis de Sales, who used his skill as a writer to reach the hearts and the minds of the people of his day, is the patron saint of journalists.

SAINT OF THE MONTH
St. John Bosco (1815-1888)

We are often upset with adolescents because they appear to be daydreaming. John Bosco was a dreamer. But instead of being told to "knock it off," John was told by Pope Pius IX, "Write down these dreams and everything else you have told me, minutely and in their natural sense."

When he was nine, John began having dreams that would guide him. From a dream in which children were transformed from wild beasts into lambs, he recognized his vocation to work with troubled youth. He learned to juggle and to do tricks to get their attention. Once he had the attention of poor, neglected, or troubled youth, he would talk with them, minister to them, and encourage them to go to Mass.

Doesn't sound too different from youth ministry today, does it?

The Church honors St. John Bosco on January 31.

CELEBRATING OUR HOLY FAMILIES

ON YOUR MARK!

- To remind young people that the Church ends December by celebrating the Feast of the Holy Family and begins January by celebrating Mary the Mother of God
- To enable young people to understand how family heritage influences who they are

GET SET!

- Display the Bible, opened to Matthew 1:1-17, in your prayer space.
- Ask the group to line up and count off by twos. Then ask the Number Ones and the Number Twos to stand opposite one another. The Number Ones will find their partners facing them. Ask young people to form pairs.
- Provide copies of **Handout 3: The Genealogy of Jesus Christ**, one copy for each person.
- Give each pair two sheets of newsprint and felt-tipped markers.
- Provide copies of **Handout 4: Creating a Family Crest**, one copy for each person. If possible provide brightly colored tagboard about 3' x 2', one sheet for each participant. Ask teens to draw on their tagboard a large copy of the crest on **Handout 4**. If it is not possible to provide tagboard for teens, copy **Handout 4** on brightly colored 8 ½" x 11" sheets of paper.

GO!

- Ask a young person to read aloud Matthew 1:1-17.
- Make sure that young people know that genealogy is a record of the ancestry of a person. It is a family tree. Then explain that today the young people are going to work in pairs to graph the genealogy of Jesus. They can use a simple linear graph to do this. Provide an example of the beginning of this tree for everyone. See **Handout 5: Jesus' Family Tree**.
- Explain that Matthew's Gospel presents Jesus as the climax of the history of Israel. Ask young people to take their copies of **Handouts 3** and **5** home as models of how family history is traced. Ask them to work backward from when they were adopted or born into their family to trace their family history. Foster children can trace the history of their birth family or the family they are living with now. It is important that you make suggestions for how this activity can be adapted to the different family situations of young people in your group. Tell teens that their family trees will not be collected. The activity is a challenge for them to see how far they can go in tracing their own family histories.
- Using the crest on **Handout 4**, ask young people to create a family crest with the person or persons they are currently living with. Explain that the crests will be shared with the entire group and will serve as a way for each young person to introduce his or her family to the group.

39

Handout 3   The Genealogy of Jesus Christ

Abraham was the father of Isaac, and Isaac was the father of Jacob. Jacob was the father of Judah and his brothers. Judah was the father of Perez and Zerah, whose mother was Tamar. Perez was the father of Hezron, and Hezron was the father of Aram. Aram was the father of Aminadab, and Aminadab was the father of Nahshon. Nahshon was the father of Salmon, and Salmon was the father of Boaz, whose mother was Rahab. Boaz became the father of Obed, whose mother was Ruth. Obed became the father of Jesse, the father of King David.

David became the father of Solomon, whose mother was Bathsheba. Solomon was the father of Rehoboam, and Rehoboam was the father of Abijah. Abijah was the father of Asaph, and Asaph was the father of Jehoshaphat. Jehoshaphat was the father of Joram, and Joram was the father of Uzziah. Uzziah was the father of Jotham, and Jotham was the father of Ahaz. Ahaz was the father of Hezekiah, and Hezekiah became the father of Manasseh. Manasseh was the father of Amos, and Amos was the father of Josiah. Josiah became the father of Jechoniah and his brothers at the time of the Babylonian exile.

After the Babylonian exile, Jechoniah became the father of Salathiel, and Salathiel was the father of Zerubbabel. Zerubbabel was the father of Abiud, and Abiud was the father of Eliakim. Eliakim was the father of Azor, and Azor was the father of Zadok. Zadok became the father of Achim, and Achim was the father of Eliud. Eliud was the father of Eleazar, and Eleazar became the father of Matthan. Matthan was the father of Jacob, and Jacob was the father of Joseph, the husband of Mary, the mother of Jesus.

There were fourteen generations from Abraham to David, fourteen generations from David to the Babylonian exile, and fourteen generations from the Babylonian exile to Jesus.

—adapted from Matthew 1:1-17

Handout 4 ✿ Creating a Family Crest

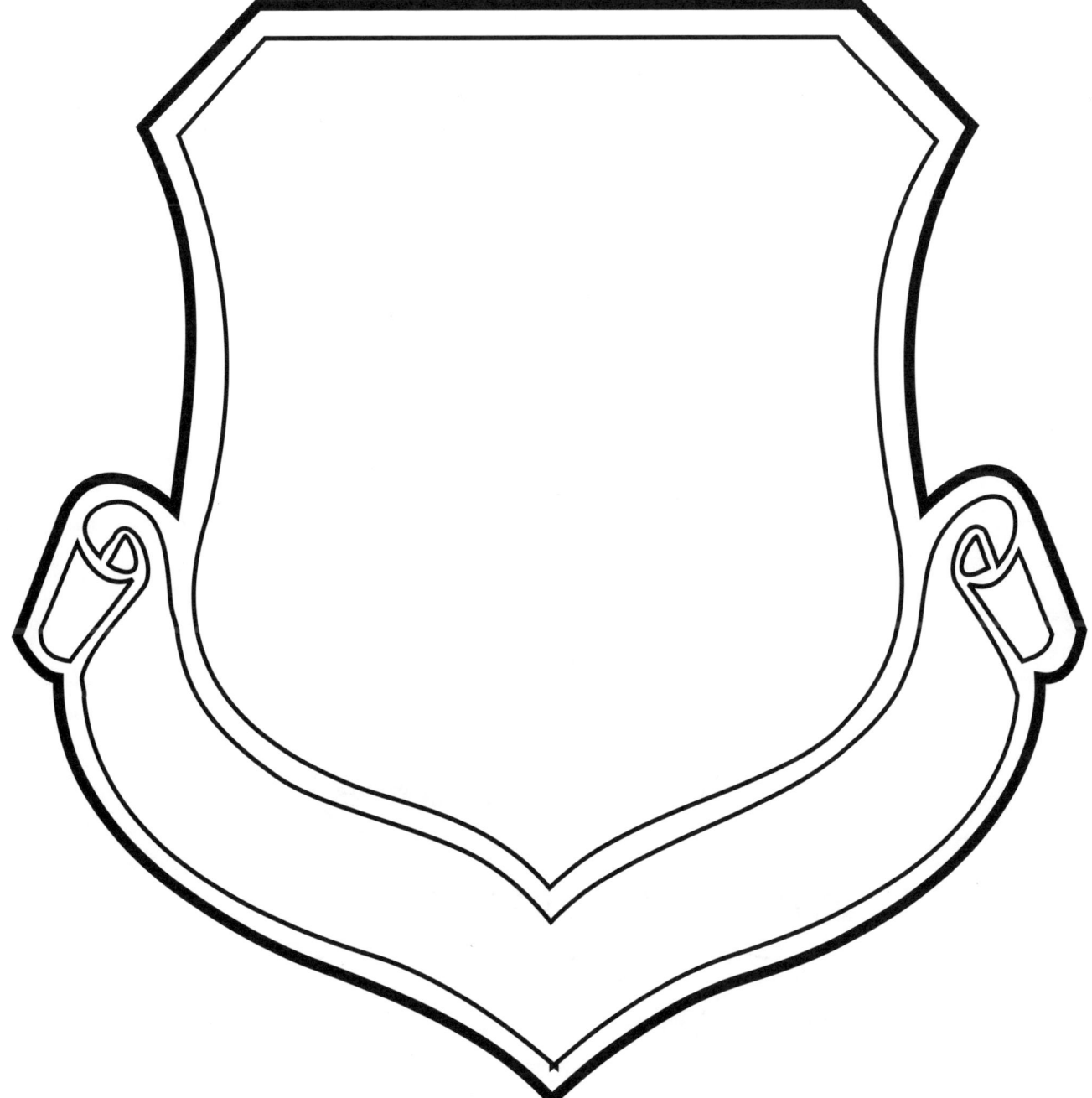

When we reflect on holiness, the first place we look is to the family. It is in our families that our growth in holiness can be nurtured.

As a family, work to create a crest that shows how your family is special. Include objects and words that reflect:

- Your family heritage
- The blends that are in your family
- The contribution of each family member
- Your family values and faith
- Activities that you do as family

Thank you for participating in this family activity!

©2002 Pflaum Publishing Group, Dayton, OH 45439 (800-543-4383). Permission is granted by the publisher to reproduce this page for educational use only.

Handout 5 — Jesus' Family Tree

- ABRAHAM
  - ISAAC
    - JACOB
      - JUDAH / and HIS BROTHERS
        - PEREZ
          - HEZRON
        - ZERAH

ANOINTING AT THE MOVIES

ON YOUR MARK!

- To serve as a springboard for a discussion of the sacrament of the Anointing of the Sick

NOW PLAYING
PATCH ADAMS

GET SET!

- Rent the video *Patch Adams*.
- Prepare to show the scene right after Carin's funeral.

GO!

- Introduce the movie. In the scene that you are about to show, two women play an important role. The first is Mrs. Kennedy, an elderly woman who wishes to one day swim in a bowl full of noodles. The other woman is Patch's friend Carin, who has just died. Men had abused Carin in the past, and this abuse made Carin envy caterpillars. She explained, "No matter what they were before, or what happened to them, they could just hide away and turn into these beautiful creatures that could fly away completely untouched."

- Show the scene, ending after Mrs. Kennedy swims in the noodles and Patch walks away.
- Explain that today the group will be talking about a sacrament of healing, the sacrament of the Anointing of the Sick. Ask these or similar questions:

Which of the characters in this scene is in need of healing?

What kinds of healing are necessary for the people in this scene?

Do you believe that God can heal people miraculously? Why or why not?

Why do people often come to church when they are seriously ill? What do you think they are seeking?

Do you know someone who is seriously ill? Who?

Have you ever been anointed? Do you know someone else who has been?

JANUARY DISCUSSION STARTER: THE PARK

ON YOUR MARK!
- To encourage young people to be inclusive
- To give young people the opportunity to see the creativity that can be achieved when they work together

GET SET!
- Read the scenario yourself.
- Adapt the number of roles to the size of your group. If your group is large, ask young people to form two or more groups for this activity. If your group is small, reduce the number of roles.
- Have young people choose roles to take in a discussion of the scenario.
- Provide paper, markers, and other materials needed for designing the park. Shoeboxes could provide the framework for the groups' designs. Work with whatever materials are available.
- Read, or have a volunteer read, the scenario to the group.

GO!

SCENARIO
A prominent citizen of your town has died. In her will, she left 320 acres of land to "be used for a magnificent park, as long as all the voters approve of its use." If the residents of the town cannot agree on how to use the land, the property will be turned over to the citizen's cat, Pretty Boy.

Nearly three quarters of the town's residents support the park development. The problem is that different groups have different ideas about how to use the park land. To mention just a few of these ideas, senior citizens want benches and shuffleboard courts, teenagers want ramps for skateboards, and sports enthusiasts want baseball and football fields.

GATHERED AROUND THE DISCUSSION TABLE ARE:
- The park planner who needs to make sure every suggestion is included
- A representative of the senior citizens
- A parent of pre-school children
- A high school youth
- A person who thinks that a butterfly museum should be included
- A neighbor who is concerned about the noise and traffic the park will create
- A person with physical disabilities who wants to make sure that the park will be accessible

YOUR TASK:
- Design a park that will meet the needs of every group so that the town's voters can agree on its use.

Notes for Group Leaders
In the **Discussion Starter**, teens are encouraged to take on the roles of persons involved in this situation. They are "acting" in the initial discussion.

What is most important is to bring the discussion to a conclusion. After the discussion, ask young people to shift away from their roles and return to being themselves. Help teens to process the experience by asking questions such as these:

- What values are involved in this scenario?
- What Catholic teachings can be applied?
- How are those involved in this situation called to be Christ?

Young people deserve to be so much more than actors with roles: they are disciples of Christ, learning how to take faith into the community!

FEBRUARY

FEBRUARY-AT-A-GLANCE

February was named for a Roman festival of purification, *Februa*.

FEBRUARY FROM A CATHOLIC CHRISTIAN PERSPECTIVE

In February we celebrate purification in the Feast of the Presentation. In the time of Jesus, Jewish women were kept in a state of semi-seclusion for forty days following the birth of a son. So, if you mark December 25 as Day 1, December 26 as Day 2, and so on, then Day 40 is February 2. To return to the community, Mary would offer a sacrifice for her purification and, at the same time, present her son to the Lord.

The Catholic Church celebrates the Feast of the Presentation on February 2, the day on which Joseph and Mary would have brought the baby Jesus to the temple.

> When the time came for their purification according to the law of Moses, they brought him up to Jerusalem to present him to the Lord (as it is written in the law of the Lord, "Every firstborn male shall be designated as holy to the Lord"), and they offered a sacrifice according to what is stated in the law of the Lord, "a pair of turtledoves or two young pigeons."
>
> Now there was a man in Jerusalem whose name was Simeon; this man was righteous and devout, looking forward to the consolation of Israel, and the Holy Spirit rested on him. It had been revealed to him by the Holy Spirit that he would not see death before he had seen the Lord's Messiah. Guided by the Spirit, Simeon came into the temple; and when the parents brought in the child Jesus, to do for him what was customary under the law, Simeon took him in his arms and praised God, saying,
>
> > "Master, now you are dismissing your servant in peace,
> >   according to your word;
> > for my eyes have seen your salvation,
> >   which you have prepared in the presence of all the peoples,
> > a light for revelation to the Gentiles
> >   and for glory to your people Israel."
>
> And the child's father and mother were amazed at what was being said about him. Then Simeon blessed them and said to his mother Mary, "This child is destined for the falling and rising of many in Israel, and to be a sign that will be opposed so that the inner thoughts of many will be revealed—and a sword will pierce your own soul too."
>
> Luke 2:22-35

SAINT OF THE MONTH
St. Blaise (d. 316)

Catholics celebrate the Feast of St. Blaise on February 3. Those who work with children would do well to recall why we bless throats on that day. Legend has it that a child had a fishbone stuck in his throat. The boy was brought to Blaise, who healed him. Catholics now celebrate the Feast of St. Blaise by having their throats blessed. Two blessed candles are held against our throats or over our heads while we pray to God through the intercession of St. Blaise to bless our throats.

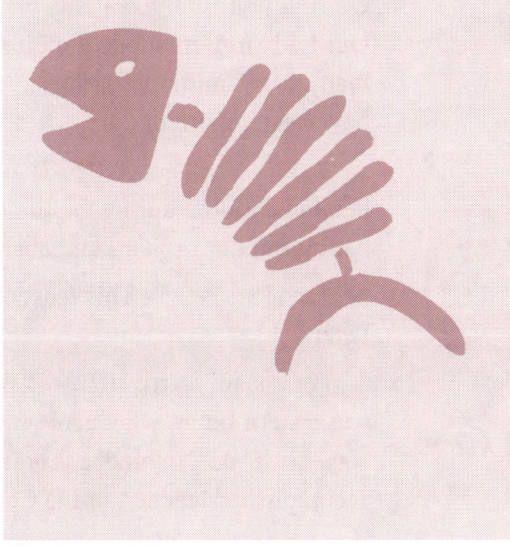

SNOW GLOBES

ON YOUR MARK!

- To enable young people to appreciate God's gift of forgiveness
- To help young people see the sacrament of Penance as a great gift from God

GET SET!

- Collect baby-food jars, one for each participant. Paint the lid of each jar so that it is all one color. Allow the paint to dry completely.
- You will also need:

  A hot glue gun (or more than one if you have a large group)
  Epoxy glue
  Small plastic people, animals, trees
  Aquarium gravel
  Iridescent glitter
  Water
  Food coloring
  Spray paint

- Make copies of **Handout 6: Making Snow Globes**, one for each participant. Make enough copies of **Handout 7: Isaiah 1:18** so that each participant will have a copy of the Scripture passage.

GO!

- Talk about the sacrament of Penance in the context of Lent, a time when we examine our lives. Explain that Lent is a time for us to see how we line up with God's will for our lives. We celebrate what we do well and look for opportunities to enhance these accomplishments. We search out where we miss the mark and look for opportunities to be reconciled with God.

  Remind young people that there is nothing that can separate them from the love of God. Tell them that they are going to make snow globes to serve as a reminder of how God sees us when we are repentant.

- Provide copies of **Handout 6**, the instructions for making snow globes, one for each young person. Make sure that young people know they can ask for help.
- When the snow globes are done, read aloud Isaiah 1:18. Ask young people to discuss what they think this passage means. When everyone has had a chance to contribute to the discussion, have teens glue a copy of the passage from Isaiah to the top of the lid of their globes.
- Make sure teens check to see that the lids are tightened before turning the globes over.

GREAT CHURCH FEAST DAYS

11 Our Lady of Lourdes—This feast commemorates the appearances of Our Lady to Bernadette Soubirous in Lourdes, France, in 1858. As many as six million pilgrims a year visit Lourdes, where many miracles have been reported.

20 St. Jerome Emiliani (d. 1537)—Because of St. Jerome's devotion to helping children during the time of the plague, he is considered the patron saint of orphans and abandoned children.

22 Chair of St. Peter—This feast celebrates the role and authority of St. Peter.

23 St. Peter Damian (d. 1072)—Like John the Baptist, St. Peter Damian was a stern figure whose role was to call people from the error of their ways to virtue. An eloquent preacher, he was named a doctor, or accomplished teacher, of the Church.

Handout 6  Making Snow Globes

Be careful!

Use the hot glue gun to glue gravel, plastic people, trees, and animals to the inside of the lid of your jar.

Pour water into the jar until it is almost full.

Spoon some glitter into the water.

Use epoxy glue to fasten the lid onto the jar.

Wait for the glue to dry.

Wait for additional instructions.

Handout 7 — Isaiah 1:18

"Though your sins are like scarlet, they shall be like snow." Isaiah 1:18	"Though your sins are like scarlet, they shall be like snow." Isaiah 1:18	"Though your sins are like scarlet, they shall be like snow." Isaiah 1:18
"Though your sins are like scarlet, they shall be like snow." Isaiah 1:18	"Though your sins are like scarlet, they shall be like snow." Isaiah 1:18	"Though your sins are like scarlet, they shall be like snow." Isaiah 1:18
"Though your sins are like scarlet, they shall be like snow." Isaiah 1:18	"Though your sins are like scarlet, they shall be like snow." Isaiah 1:18	"Though your sins are like scarlet, they shall be like snow." Isaiah 1:18
"Though your sins are like scarlet, they shall be like snow." Isaiah 1:18	"Though your sins are like scarlet, they shall be like snow." Isaiah 1:18	"Though your sins are like scarlet, they shall be like snow." Isaiah 1:18
"Though your sins are like scarlet, they shall be like snow." Isaiah 1:18	"Though your sins are like scarlet, they shall be like snow." Isaiah 1:18	"Though your sins are like scarlet, they shall be like snow." Isaiah 1:18
"Though your sins are like scarlet, they shall be like snow." Isaiah 1:18	"Though your sins are like scarlet, they shall be like snow." Isaiah 1:18	"Though your sins are like scarlet, they shall be like snow." Isaiah 1:18

RECONCILIATION: A COUNTERCULTURAL IDEA

ON YOUR MARK!

- To enable young people to see that sometimes reconciliation and peacemaking are countercultural
- To expose young people to the Gospel challenge to reconciliation that is present in their everyday lives

GET SET!

- List these eight statements on newsprint and post the newsprint where everyone can see it.
- Copy **Handout 8: God's Word Speaks to Us**. Cut the Scripture passages apart, with one passage on each slip of paper. Make sure there are enough slips so that each young person can have one or two Scripture passages. More than one person can have the same passages.
- Have masking tape available for young people to share.

1. Get all you can!
2. You have to look out for Number One!
3. Don't get mad. Get even!
4. I really didn't want to help, but volunteering will look good on college applications.
5. Don't get involved!
6. It's a dog-eat-dog world. Let everyone look out for themselves. It's survival of the fittest!
7. It's not my problem!
8. The poor are lazy!

GO!

- Ask young people for examples of circumstances in which they have heard the statements on the newsprint used, or in which they could imagine the statements being used. After everyone has had a chance to contribute to the discussion, distribute the Scripture passages from **Handout 8** to the group. Have masking tape available.
- Explain that the Scripture passages relate to the statements on the newsprint. Ask teens to match their Scripture passages with the statements. Read aloud a statement from the newsprint, and ask which young person has a Scripture passage that relates to the statement. When someone offers an appropriate response, have that person tape the Scripture passage over the statement on newsprint. See **Handout 9: Answer Key** for appropriate responses.
- When all statements and Scripture passages have been matched, explain that it sometimes seems as if there are voices whispering to us from all sides—the media, parents, teachers, the Gospel, friends, daily temptations, Jesus. Eventually we need to answer the 5-W question: **Which whisper within will win?** Write this question where everyone can see it, and point out that God calls each of us to be a reconciling voice in a world that needs reconciliation. Give teens time to talk about some of the conflicting voices they hear in their lives.

Handout 8   God's Word Speaks to Us

Sell your possessions, and give alms. Make purses for yourselves that do not wear out, an unfailing treasure in heaven, where no thief comes near and no moth destroys. For where your treasure is, there your heart will be also.
                                    Luke 12:33-34

You shall love your neighbor as yourself.
                                  Matthew 22:39

But many who are first will be last, and the last will be first.
                                  Matthew 19:30

So whenever you give alms, do not sound a trumpet before you, as the hypocrites do in the synagogues and in the streets, so that they may be praised by others. Truly I tell you, they have received their reward. But when you give alms, do not let your left hand know what your right hand is doing, so that your alms may be done in secret; and your Father who sees in secret will reward you.
                                  Matthew 6:2-4

But I say to you that listen, Love your enemies, do good to those who hate you, bless those who curse you, pray for those who abuse you.
                                  Luke 6:27-28

Truly I tell you, just as you did it to one of the least of these who are members of my family, you did it to me.
                                  Matthew 25:40

Everyone therefore who acknowledges me before others, I also will acknowledge before my Father in heaven; but whoever denies me before others, I also will deny before my Father in heaven.
                                  Matthew 10:32-33

Blessed are the poor in spirit, for theirs is the kingdom of heaven.
                                  Matthew 5:3

Handout 9 ✎ Answer Key

1. Get all you can!
   Scripture response: Luke 12:33-34

2. You have to look out for Number One!
   Scripture response: Matthew 19:30

3. Don't get mad. Get even!
   Scripture response: Luke 6:27-28

4. I really didn't want to help, but volunteering will look good on college applications.
   Scripture response: Matthew 6:2-4

5. Don't get involved!
   Scripture response: Matthew 10:32-33

6. It's a dog-eat-dog world. Let everyone look out for themselves. It's survival of the fittest!
   Scripture response: Matthew 22:39

7. It's not my problem!
   Scripture response: Matthew 25:40

8. The poor are lazy!
   Scripture response: Matthew 5:3

MATRIMONY AT THE MOVIES

ON YOUR MARK!
- To provide a springboard for a discussion of the sacrament of Matrimony

GET SET!
- Rent the video *Father of the Bride* (1991).
- Preview the video from the scene in which the viewer learns that Annie is coming home to the end of the first basketball scene.

GO!
- Show the scenes from the video.
- Ask these or similar questions.

  What values of marriage does the movie point out?

  How does George feel about his married life?

  What are his daughter's concerns?

  What changes Annie's mind?

  What did she admire about her fiancé?

  Does George remind you of your parent or parents? Why? In what ways?

FEBRUARY DISCUSSION STARTER: THE PHARMACY

ON YOUR MARK!
To help young people:
- See the need to make decisions based on moral principles
- Develop problem-solving skills
- Understand that people are more important than things

GET SET!
- Read the scenario yourself.
- Adapt the number of roles to the size of your group. If your group is large, ask young people to form two or more groups for this activity. If your group is small, reduce the number of roles.
- Have young people choose roles to take in a discussion of the scenario.
- Read, or have a volunteer read, the scenario aloud to the group.

GO!

SCENARIO
A small, independently owned pharmacy has been experiencing increased competition in its suburban location. Two large, national chains are building huge new drugstores in the area. Even the grocery stores have added pharmacies. But the small pharmacy has a good reputation in the community. Customers feel that the management has always looked out for the good of the customers, and they have remained loyal.

A group from the local high school, including one of the pharmacy's part-time employees, and members of the American Cancer

Society have started to picket the store. The picketers are protesting the fact that the pharmacy sells tobacco products. They are especially concerned about the increasing numbers of teenagers who smoke.

The owner of the pharmacy understands the protesters' point. It is difficult for him to say that he cares about the health of his customers and still sell cigarettes. But the reality is that twenty percent of nonpharmaceutical revenue comes from the sale of cigarettes. If he didn't sell cigarettes and other tobacco products, he would have to raise drug prices. That would hurt all his customers, especially the poor and the elderly. He might be forced to close his store if he can't keep his prices competitive with those of the large chain stores and the grocery stores.

Notes for Group Leaders

In the *Discussion Starter*, teens take on the roles of persons involved in this situation. They are "acting" in the initial discussion.

What is most important is to bring the discussion to a conclusion. After the discussion, ask young people to shift away from their roles and return to being themselves. Help teens to process the experience by asking questions such as these:

- What values are involved in this scenario?
- What Catholic teachings can be applied?
- How are those involved in this situation called to be Christ?

Young people deserve to be so much more than actors with roles: they are disciples of Christ, learning how to take faith to the marketplace!

GATHERED AT THE DISCUSSION TABLE ARE:

- The pharmacy owner
- The pharmacist, who is concerned about losing his job and income
- The part-time worker who has joined the picketers
- A youth who buys cigarettes and considers it his right to decide whether or not to smoke
- An American Cancer Society member who lost his spouse to lung cancer
- A worker who could lose her job if the pharmacy makes cuts
- A cigarette vendor who knows that if people can't buy their cigarettes at the drugstore, they will just buy them somewhere else.

YOUR TASK:

- Help the owner of the pharmacy make a decision about whether or not to sell cigarettes. The owner can ask each person questions.
- Come up with a solution that takes into account the concerns of each person at the table.

MARCH

MARCH-AT-A-GLANCE

March was named for Mars, the father of Romulus and Remus, the mythic twins who were responsible for the founding of Rome. Mars was also considered the god of war and the guardian of the state.

MARCH FROM A CATHOLIC CHRISTIAN PERSPECTIVE

Catholics do not celebrate the god of war. In March, we celebrate the Prince of Peace. Catholics celebrate the Feast of the Annunciation on March 25, nine months before December 25. We celebrate Mary's "yes" to God.

GREAT CHURCH FEAST DAYS

4   St. Casimir of Poland (d. 1484)—Called "The Peacemaker" by Poles, St. Casimir is the patron saint of Poland and Lithuania.

4   Sts. Perpetua and Felicity and their Companions (d. 203)—During a persecution of Christians, Sts. Perpetua and Felicity and their companions were imprisoned and sentenced to face wild beasts. Sts. Perpetua and Felicity both survived the attack of a wild animal and were then stabbed by gladiators.

9   St. Frances of Rome (d. 1440)—Without neglecting her duties to her husband and children, this gentle saint dedicated herself to helping the poor of Rome. She formed a society of women who, without taking religious vows, offered themselves to God and to serving the poor.

17 St. Patrick (d. 461)—This saint's intense love of God allowed him to convert Ireland to Christianity. He is Ireland's patron.

19 St. Joseph, husband of Blessed Virgin Mary (first century)—We know very little about St. Joseph, except that he was trusted with a very important role—protector of Mary and Jesus. Probably because Joseph was a carpenter, he is considered the patron of workers.

23 St. Turibius of Lima (d. 1606)—As Archbishop of Lima, St. Turibius is said to have confirmed three other saints—St. Rose of Lima, St. Martin de Porres, and St. John Massias.

25 The Annunciation of the Lord—This feast commemorates the announcement by the angel Gabriel that Mary was to give birth to the Son of God and, with that, Mary's free acceptance of her role.

SAINT OF THE MONTH

St. Katharine Drexel (1858-1955)

Katharine Drexel was a Philadelphia socialite who inherited millions of dollars. She caused quite a stir in polite Philadelphia society when she decided to use her millions for those who were not given access to education. The "million-heiress" entered religious life and founded an order dedicated to serving Native and African Americans. A champion of social justice in the Church, she worked tirelessly for integration and education. The life of St. Katharine Drexel reminds each of us to share our "fortunes" with those who are marginalized. We celebrate her life on her feast day, March 3.

FEAST OF THE ANNUNCIATION

ON YOUR MARK!

- To help young people learn about the Feast of the Annunciation

GET SET!

- Review the birth announcements that are included in this activity.
- Make copies of **Handout 10: Announcing the Birth of John the Baptist** for half of the group. For the other half of the group make copies of **Handout 11: Announcing the Birth of Jesus**.
- Copy **Handout 12: A "Mom" Quiz for John the Baptist**, one copy for each participant who received the birth announcement for John.
- Copy **Handout 13: A "Mom" Quiz for Jesus**, one copy for everyone who received the birth announcement for Jesus.
- Have a flip chart and markers available.

GO!

- Provide teens with basic information about the Feast of the Annunciation, which is celebrated on March 25. This is nine months before December 25, the date on which the Church celebrates the birth of Jesus. The Feast of the Annunciation celebrates the announcement that Mary is going to have a baby named Jesus. The feast also celebrates Mary's "yes" to God—her acceptance of God's difficult plan for her life.
- Mary's cousin Elizabeth was pregnant when Mary heard the news about her own pregnancy. Explain that this activity will look at the birth of Elizabeth's baby, John the Baptist, and the birth of Jesus, to see what the births have in common and how they differ.
- Give half of the group **Handout 10: Announcing the Birth of John the Baptist** and the other half of the group **Handout 11: Announcing the Birth of Jesus**. Give teens time to read their announcements.
- Then explain that there will be an open-book quiz on what teens have read. They will be able to find the answers to the quiz questions in the announcements.
- Those who read the announcement of the birth of John will need **Handout 12: A "Mom" Quiz for John the Baptist**. Those who read the announcement of the birth of Jesus will need **Handout 13: A "Mom" Quiz for Jesus**.
- Divide both groups into smaller groups, probably two or three persons each, to answer the quiz questions. One member of each group should record the group's answers on the handout.
- While the teens are working, circulate among the groups to see how they are doing. If teens get stuck and do not know the answer to a question, point out that the answers to the quiz questions are italicized in the birth announcements.
- Divide a sheet of newsprint on the flip chart into two columns, one labeled **John the Baptist** and the other labeled **Jesus**.
- When the groups are finished with their quizzes, bring participants back together into one large group. Ask the quiz questions out loud and write the answers teens give on the newsprint so that participants can compare and contrast the birth of John with the birth of Jesus. This exercise should help them see that while the births of John and Jesus were very similar, there were also some significant differences. **Handout 14** provides an answer key.

Handout 10
Announcing the Birth of John the Baptist!

In the days of King Herod of Judea, there was a priest named Zechariah, who belonged to the priestly order of Abijah. His wife was a descendant of Aaron, and her name was Elizabeth. Both of them were righteous before God, living blamelessly according to all the commandments and regulations of the Lord. But they had no children, because ***Elizabeth was barren, and both were getting on in years***.

Once when he was serving as priest before God and his section was on duty, he was chosen by lot, according to the custom of the priesthood, to enter the sanctuary of the Lord and offer incense. Now at the time of the incense offering, the whole assembly of the people was praying outside. Then ***there appeared to him an angel of the Lord***, standing at the right side of the altar of incense. When Zechariah saw him, ***he was terrified; and fear overwhelmed him***. But the angel said to him, ***"Do not be afraid***, Zechariah, for your prayer has been heard. ***Your wife Elizabeth will bear you a son***, and you will name him John. You will have joy and gladness, and many will rejoice at his birth, for ***he will be great in the sight of the Lord***. He must never drink wine or strong drink; even before his birth he will be filled with the Holy Spirit. He will turn many of the people of Israel to the Lord their God. With the spirit and the power of Elijah he will go before him, to turn the hearts of parents to their children, and the disobedient to the wisdom of the righteous, to make ready a people prepared for the Lord." Zechariah said to the angel, ***"How will I know that this is so?*** For I am an old man, and my wife is getting on in years." The angel replied, "I am Gabriel. I stand in the presence of God, and ***I have been sent to speak to you and to bring you this good news***. But now, because you did not believe my words, which will be fulfilled in their time, ***you will become mute, unable to speak***, until the day these things occur."

Meanwhile the people were waiting for Zechariah, and wondering at his delay in the sanctuary. When he did come out, ***he could not speak*** to them, and they realized that he had seen a vision in the sanctuary. He kept motioning to them and remained unable to speak. When his time of service was ended, he went to his home.

After those days his wife Elizabeth conceived, and for five months she remained in seclusion. She said, "This is what the Lord has done for me when he looked favorably on me and took away the disgrace I have endured among my people."

Luke 1:5–25

Handout 11
Announcing the Birth of Jesus!

In the sixth month *the angel Gabriel* was sent by God to a town in Galilee called Nazareth, *to a virgin engaged to a man whose name was Joseph*, of the house of David. The virgin's name was Mary. And he came to her, and said, "Greetings, favored one! The Lord is with you." But *she was much perplexed* by his words and pondered what sort of greeting this might be. The angel said to her, *"Do not be afraid, Mary, for you have found favor with God.* And now, *you will conceive in your womb and bear a son, and you will name him Jesus. He will be great, and will be called the Son of the Most High, and the Lord God will give to him the throne of his ancestor David. He will reign over the house of Jacob forever, and of his kingdom there will be no end."* Mary said to the angel, *"How can this be, since I am a virgin?"* The angel said to her, *"The Holy Spirit will come upon you,* and the power of the Most High will overshadow you: therefore the child to be born will be holy: he will be called Son of God. And now, *your relative Elizabeth in her old age has also conceived a son*; and this is the sixth month for her who was said to be barren. For nothing will be impossible with God." *Then Mary said, "Here am I, the servant of the Lord; let it be with me according to your word."* Then the angel departed from her.

Luke 1:26-38

Handout 12   A "Mom" Quiz* for John the Baptist

1. Were the parents planning to have a child? Why or why not?

2. Who appears to Zechariah?

3. What is Zechariah's initial response when the angel appears?

4. What does the angel say to Zechariah in response?

5. The angel drops some big news on Zechariah. What is the angel's news? And what will the news be named?

6. What will this child be in the sight of the Lord?

7. What does Zechariah ask?

8. What is the angel's response?

9. What is the sign given to Zechariah?

10. What is Zechariah's response?

*To balance all the "Pop" quizzes you've had

Handout 13   A "Mom" Quiz* for Jesus

1. Were the parents planning to have a child? Why or why not?

2. Who appears to Mary?

3. What is Mary's initial response when the angel appears?

4. What does the angel say to Mary in response?

5. The angel drops some big news on Mary. What is the angel's news? And what will the news be named?

6. What will the child be in the sight of the Lord?

7. What does Mary ask?

8. What is the angel's response?

9. What is the sign given to Mary?

10. What is Mary's response?

*To balance all the "Pop" quizzes you've had

Handout 14 — Answer Key for the "Mom" Quizzes

Question	John the Baptist	Jesus
Were the parents planning to have a child? Why or why not?	No. Elizabeth was barren, and both were getting on in years.	No. Joseph and Mary were not married, and Mary was a virgin.
Who appears to Zechariah/to Mary?	An angel of the Lord	The angel Gabriel
What is Zechariah's/Mary's initial response when the angel appears?	Zechariah was overwhelmed by fear.	Mary was perplexed.
What does the angel say about this response?	"Do not be afraid."	"Do not be afraid, Mary, for you have found favor with God."
The angel drops some big news. What is the angel's news? And what will the news be named?	"Your wife Elizabeth will bear you a son, and you will name him John."	"You will conceive in your womb and bear a son, and you will name him Jesus."
What will the child be in the sight of the Lord?	"He will be great in the sight of the Lord."	"He will be great, and will be called Son of the Most High, and the Lord God will give to him the throne of his ancestor David. He will reign over the house of Jacob forever, and of his kingdom there will be no end."
What does Zechariah/Mary ask?	"How will I know that this is so?"	"How can this be, since I am a virgin?"
What is the angel's response?	"I have been sent to speak to you and to bring you this good news."	"The Holy Spirit will come upon you."
What is the sign given to Zechariah/Mary?	"You will become mute, unable to speak."	"Your relative Elizabeth in her old age has also conceived a son."
What is Zechariah's/Mary's response?	Zechariah could not speak.	Then Mary said, "Here I am, the servant of the Lord; let it be with me according to your word."

A LENTEN CHALLENGE: ENTER THE PASSION

ON YOUR MARK!

- To enable young people to focus on the cross of Jesus
- To help teens discover the meaning of the cross for our lives

GET SET!

- Make, or have someone make, crosses to remind young people to enter the passion. Use 2" x 3" boards and cut them into five-inch blocks. Then use a dado blade or a router to cut a cross about one-half inch deep in each block. Sand the cross so there are no rough edges. Make enough blocks with crosses in them so that each young person can receive one.
- Have paints or markers available for each young person.
- Arrange all of the crosses around a crucifix in your prayer space.

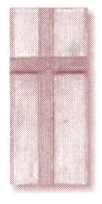
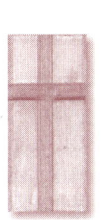

GO!

- Tell teens that Lent is a time when we meditate on the meaning of the cross of Christ. The cross is a paradox for us—the instrument of death is a sign of life. The cross stands as a sign of the depth of God's love for us. Our suffering and pain—our own cross—find meaning in the pain and suffering of Jesus Christ on the cross.
- Distribute the crosses.
- Ask each participant to think of people who are experiencing suffering—themselves, a grandparent, the hungry and homeless, those on death row, or those living in a country ravaged by war, disease, or natural disaster. Then ask teens to decorate their crosses so that a suffering person or group is represented. They can use words or symbols.
- Remind teens that Jesus said, "And I, when I am lifted up from the earth, will draw all people to myself" (John 12:32). Ask teens to touch their crosses to the crucifix and follow that prayerful action by praying for the suffering person or persons they are thinking of. Also remind them that this action is a sign of the importance of uniting all suffering to the cross of Christ.
- Have teens pray intercessions out loud. For example:

We pray for persons who have Alzheimer's, and especially for my grandmother.

I pray for my brother Chris, and all who are victims of violence.

I pray for all prisoners who are on death row, and all victims of crimes that they may have committed.

LENTEN PRACTICE: LOVING PEOPLE, NOT THINGS

ON YOUR MARK!

- To help young people examine the Lenten practice of fasting from things that distract us from God and God's ways
- To encourage young people to reach out to others during Lent—to attach to people and detach from things

GET SET!

- Invite a group of children to meet with your group of teens. Make sure you have one teen to work with each child for this activity.
- For each child, you will need:

  An eight- to twelve-inch terra cotta tray, the kind that goes under a terra cotta pot.

  Enough potting soil to fill the trays one-third full

  Enough small stones to fill the trays one-third full

  One paper-white narcissus bulb

  Two zip-lock plastic bags

- Place the soil in individual bags. Each bag should contain enough soil to fill one-third of a terra cotta tray.
- Place the stones in individual bags. Each bag should contain enough stones to fill one-third of a terra cotta tray.
- Optional: Have a teen who is artistic prepare a storybook by adding pictures for every three or four verses of the story of the people of the Clan Potsontheground on **Handout 15**.

GO!

- Explain to the young people ahead of time that a group of children will be joining them for a special Lenten gathering, where they will help to teach the children about the importance of Lent and about the discipline of detaching from things and attaching to people.
- Ask for volunteers to serve as storytellers. Provide the storytellers with copies of the story on **Handout 15: The People of the Clan Potsontheground**. Have them prepare the reading ahead of time. Encourage them to get into the spirit of the story and the season.
- Have teens help to prepare the bags of dirt and stones.
- Have the storytellers present the story. Ask teens and children to follow the directions that are part of the story.

Handout 15   The People of Clan Potsontheground*

*(pronounced pots-on-the-ground)

I have quite a story to tell you
About a far and distant nation,
But to listen to this story well,
You'll need ears and imagination.

The city I will tell you about
Is the most beautiful city on earth
And I can say that quite confidently,
For it is the city of my birth.

The people of the city were amazing.
They were called the Potsontheground Clan,
And the most amazing tribe member
Was known as Elder Wise Woman.

Elder Wise Woman was very old.
She was really quite clever and wise,
And she could make you feel better
Just by looking into your eyes.

When Elder Wise Woman spoke,
She shared wisdom that was so clear
That all members of the Potsontheground Clan
Felt better because she was near.

When children in the town turned six years old,
Elder Wise Woman would tell them the story
About the great Potsontheground people,
With all of their triumphs and glory.

It really was quite an amazing town,
Where all the people lived well.
There were no wars or crimes or violence.
There was quite a story to tell!

Elder Wise Woman would tell the story
Of the people who had known only peace.
She would speak of Potsontheground,
Where arguments and war had ceased.

She would often tell the children,
"One day, this town will be yours,
And it will be your awesome job
To keep it free from war."

"How can we do that?" the young asked.
Elder Wise Woman said, "You can start
By listening with both of your ears
And then responding from your heart."

Now sometimes that simple wisdom
Made no sense to six-year-olds,
But they remembered it anyway,
Along with stories that Wise Woman told.

There is one more thing I need to tell you—
It's unique to the Potsontheground Clan.
They shared everything they had together.
They shared their houses and their land.

The Potsontheground Clan shared their food
So that everyone would have something to eat.
And when it grew cold, they would share coats
Or share their logs for the fire's heat.

Everything belonged to everyone,
And in this town no one was greedy.
They were proud that in their tribe
There were no poor or needy.

Can you imagine living in a town
Where nothing ever went wrong?
Where all the people lived in peace,
And everyone got along!

One day things changed for the people.
A person who did evil things came to town.
This person stirred up nothing but trouble
For the people of Potsontheground.

This person was so evil,
Wise Woman called him Evil One.
This one came with a purpose,
To destroy peace before day was done.

So Evil walked among the people,
Pretending to be their friend,
And would talk and talk and talk
Till the conversation would end.

Handout 15   The People of Clan Potsontheground (page 2)

And then Evil would look at a person,
And say, "Would you like a pot?"
And Evil would give each family a bowl
That they liked really quite a lot.

Pass out the trays to the children.

After giving the bowl, Evil One said,
"Hey, now you need something to fill it.
I have some magical dirt for your bowl,
But be careful not to spill it."

Distribute the bags filled with dirt. Teens should help the children empty the dirt into their trays.

So the people of Potsontheground
Began to fill their own little pots,
And they were very careful with the dirt.
They didn't want to spill a drop.

Well, the bowls were all filled,
And the people were all pleased.
But the Evil One said aloud to all,
"I want to give you a magical seed."

Pass out the paper-white narcissus bulbs. Have teens help the children put the bulbs into the soil, cautioning them not to cover the bulbs with the soil.

So each one took the magic seed
And planted it in the magic soil,
And they were told that magic plants would grow
Because of all their hard work and toil.

The people started to look at their pots,
And they said, "This will be so pretty!
When all the plants start to grow,
We will have a most beautiful city!"

The Evil One told them they needed rocks
To protect each of their plants,
So they paid Evil money for a few stones
To keep their plants safe from insects like ants.

Pass out the bags filled with stones. Ask teens to help the children place the stones around the paper-white bulbs, making sure that the bulbs are visible through the stones.

Evil One sold stones to everyone,
Then proclaimed loud and clear,
"These rocks will work miracles,
But there is something greater you must fear."

"You must be very afraid of one another.
Protect yourself," the Evil One said.
"And in order to do this, you should—you must—
Carry your plants high, high, high above your head."

The villagers feared what others would do,
Afraid others would steal their magic dreams.
So they put their plants up on top of their heads,
Falling right into the Evil One's plans and schemes.

So they raised their arms high, high, high,
And they did just as the Evil One said.
Their arms were pressed against their ears,
They kept their arms so close to their heads.

Pretty soon the villagers grew very suspicious,
And they would stay up all night
Because they didn't want anyone to steal their plants.
That just would not be right!

Well, violence grew throughout the village,
And for the first time fights broke out.
The villagers who once trusted everyone
Now were filled with doubt.

Elder Wise Woman saw this happening,
And soft, gentle tears filled both her eyes.
She knew that the town needed help,
And she was willing to try.

Handout 15   The People of Clan Potsontheground (page 3)

"You must take the plants off your heads,
And you must stop all of this fear,"
But because their plants were being held in the air,
None of the townsfolk could hear.

None, that is, except the children,
Who listened to Wise Woman from the start,
And started to pull their parents' arms down,
And spoke from their children's heart.

They said, "All of us must stop this.
This is not the way that we should act!
People of Potsontheground, you heard
Evil lies and quoted them as fact!"

"Elder Wise Woman taught us to keep our ears open
And listen closely with all of our heart,
And begin to love people more than things again,
For that is the important part."

Elder Wise Woman listened to the children,
And her heart was filled with great joy,
For all the adults began to learn
From the little girls and boys.

The townsfolk began to treat each other well,
And be happy others were around.
And they placed their plants in the village center.
They put their pots on the ground.

That's how the people learned about the name,
This village of Potsontheground.
They learned from little children
That love makes the world go 'round.

That is one of the stories of my village,
And now it is yours, my friend.
Remember to listen with ears and with heart,
And thank you for listening. The End.

MARCH DISCUSSION STARTER: THE PUBLIC UTILITY COMPANY

ON YOUR MARK!

To help young people:
- See the need to make decisions based on moral principles
- Develop problem-solving skills
- Understand that people are more important than things

GET SET!

- Read the scenario yourself.
- Adapt the number of roles to the size of your group. If your group is large, ask young people to form two or more groups for this activity. If your group is small, reduce the number of roles.
- Have young people choose roles to take in a discussion of the scenario.
- Read, or have a volunteer read, the scenario out loud to the group.

GO!

SCENARIO

You run the local electric company, which has been very good to you. You earn the much-sought-after six-figure salary. You are admired in all the social circles, and your utility has made sizable charitable donations to many good causes. You are a popular person. Or at least you were.

Lately, all your public appearances have been marred by local activists, who shout "Murderer" at you. This began after a mother and three of her children died as they huddled around a faulty gas stove to keep warm last winter. Their electricity was turned off when they were three months behind in their payments.

Never would you have wanted anything bad to happen to that mother and her children. Yet, if everyone could get away without paying their bills, your company would be broke. Then the whole town would be without electricity. Even people who have the money don't always pay their bills on time. Turning off electrical service seems to be the only reasonable action to take when customers fail to pay their bills.

But you've lost sleep thinking about the tragedy and how it might have been prevented. So you've called together a group of advisors.

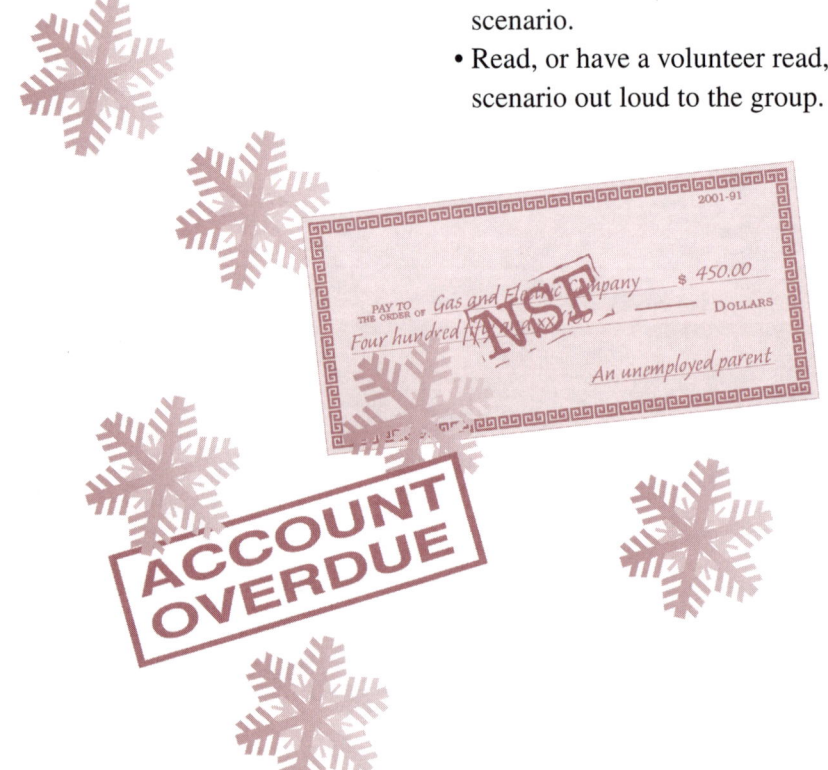

GATHERED AT THE DISCUSSION TABLE ARE:

- Two unemployed parents who stand to lose their electrical service because they are behind in their payments
- The local Catholic bishop
- Two stockholders in your company
- A representative from the mayor's office

YOUR TASK:

- Come up with a reasonable action for the utility company to take when customers fail to pay their bills.

Notes for Group Leaders

In the *Discussion Starter*, teens take on the roles of persons involved in this situation. They are "acting" in the initial discussion. It would be helpful to contact your local utility to ask what provisions have been made in your area for customers who are delinquent in their payments or unable to pay. Introduce this information into the discussion when teens have taken it as far as they can.

What is most important is to bring the discussion to a conclusion. After the discussion, ask young people to shift away from their roles and return to being themselves. Help teens to process the experience by asking questions such as these:

- What values are involved in this scenario?
- What Catholic teachings can be applied?
- How are those involved in this situation called to be Christ?

Young people deserve to be so much more than actors with roles: they are disciples of Christ, learning how to take faith to the marketplace!

APRIL

APRIL-AT-A-GLANCE

April comes from the Latin *aperire*, meaning an opening. The spring season opens, the flowers open. On the Roman calendar, the month of *Aprilis* was dedicated to Venus, the goddess of love and beauty.

APRIL FROM A CATHOLIC CHRISTIAN PERSPECTIVE

In most years, the great celebration of the Triduum takes place in April. For Catholic Christians, the Triduum is all about openings and builds to the celebration of an opening for which there is no equal. On Holy Thursday, at the Mass of the Last Supper, we celebrate Jesus' openness to serving others and his institution of the Eucharist. On Good Friday, we commemorate Jesus' opening his arms on the cross for us. At the Easter Vigil, we open welcoming arms to those who want to become Catholics, and then we triumphantly celebrate the opening of the tomb, when life wins over death!

GREAT CHURCH FEAST DAYS

✠ **Easter**—The central feast of the Christian year, Easter celebrates Christ's triumph over death in the resurrection. Easter is called a movable feast because it is celebrated the first Sunday after the first full moon of spring.

4 **St. Isidore of Seville** (d. 636)—St. Isidore believed so strongly in the value of education that he is sometimes called "The Schoolmaster of the Middle Ages." His support for education and religion made Spain a center of culture while civilization declined in the rest of Europe.

5 **St. Vincent Ferrer** (d. 1419)—On this day we remember St. Vincent Ferrer, a famous Dominican preacher. It was reported that he spoke with such energy that some in his audiences wept or fainted from fear.

13 **St. Martin I** (d. 656)—Known as an intelligent, learned, and charitable man, St. Martin became pope in 649. He is remembered as the last pope to have been martryed.

SAINT OF THE MONTH
St. John Baptist de la Salle (1651-1719)

John Baptist de la Salle was born in France to noble parents. He was an educator and an advocate for the poor. The founder of the Institute of the Brothers of the Christian Schools, John Baptist de la Salle is the patron saint of teachers and is remembered by the Church on April 7. It is good to honor those whose goal is to teach and inspire!

CHRIST DIED FOR ME!

ON YOUR MARK!

- To encourage young people to reflect on the depth of the love of Jesus Christ
- To help young people explore discipleship and what it means to be a follower of Jesus

GET SET!

- Make copies of **Handout 16: Friend to the End**, one for each participant.

GO!

- Distribute copies of **Handout 16**.
- Ask young people to list in Column One all the people they have known who have touched their lives. They may continue their lists on the back of their handouts if they need to. This list can include all the people they have had contact with as well as people they know well. Give them five minutes to create this list.
- When time is up, ask participants to circle the names of those they consider their friends. From the names they circled, ask them to write in Column Two the names of those who would do a small favor for them.
- From the names in Column Two, ask teens to write in Column Three the names of people who would do a huge favor for them.
- From the names in Column Three, ask young people to write in Column Four the names of those who would love and accept them, no matter what they did.
- In Column Four, ask teens to circle the names of the people who would give up their lives for them.
- Then bring the group together to ask what teens noticed about the activity. Ask these or similar questions.

Do you think there is anyone who would give up his or her life for you? Why?

For whom would you give up your life? Why?

- Remind teens that Jesus died for us. We know that there is no greater love possible than to lay down one's life for one's friends. Today, we see many people wearing crosses. It may seem strange to say, but wearing a cross can remind us of the way that Jesus was put to death. We need to remember that Christ died for each of us. In fact, even if each of us were the only person in the world, Jesus would still have died for each of us.

Handout 16 🙢 Friend to the End

COLUMN ONE	COLUMN TWO	COLUMN THREE	COLUMN FOUR

LOOKING AT RESURRECTION ATTITUDES

ON YOUR MARK!

- To help young people be aware of the messages that life can give
- To help them understand that the mission of Jesus is our mission

GET SET!

- For this activity, you will need a deck of playing cards, a table or other space large enough to display the complete deck, and copies of **Handout 17: Attitudes**, one for each participant.

GO!

- Introduce this activity by reminding teens that at the last supper, Jesus prayed that all would be one (John 17:21) Teens will be familiar with the fact that there are many things that keep God's people divided.
- Place all fifty-two cards of a deck face up on a table or on the floor so that everyone can see the cards. Tell young people that each playing card represents an attitude toward life.
- Distribute **Handout 17** to the participants. Ask them to read the list of attitudes. Then have each teen choose the cards from the deck that correspond to attitudes they have seen in action. The number of cards each teen may choose will depend on the size of the group.

- When all have chosen their cards (no two participants may choose the same card or attitude), have participants sit in a large circle. Ask for a volunteer to be the first player. Players are to explain why they have chosen particular cards and attitudes. Go around the circle clockwise until everyone has had a chance to share.
- After offering his or her explanation, the first player uses his or her cards to begin to construct a house of cards in the center of the group. The next player then explains his or her choices, adds to the house of cards, and so on, until all have finished. If the cards fall (and they most likely will), allow reconstruction, but make sure all participants explain the cards they have chosen.

- After everyone has had a chance to speak, allow some time for more building. If the group gets their house of cards to stand, ask how sturdy it is. What would make it fall? Ask for a volunteer to read Luke 6:46-49. Ask: What materials make a good solid foundation on which a person can build a life?

Handout 17 ✌ Attitudes

- Ace of ♥ — If I drink and drive, nothing will happen to me.
- Ace of ♦ — If you can't say something nice about a person, tell me.
- Ace of ♣ — You can never be thin enough.
- Ace of ♠ — Win at all costs.
- King of ♥ — Don't mix with people like them.
- King of ♦ — It's okay to do it—just don't get caught.
- King of ♣ — I'd do anything to get them to notice me.
- King of ♠ — School's not important. It's who you know, not what you know, that counts.
- Queen of ♥ — You'll never amount to anything!
- Queen of ♦ — I hate being _____, I'd rather be _____.
- Queen of ♣ — I hope you aren't anything like your brother or sister.
- Queen of ♠ — Do anything to get ahead.
- Jack of ♥ — We used to be best friends, but I don't talk to him or her any more.
- Jack of ♦ — I'll wait until I'm older before I get serious about religion.
- Jack of ♣ — Help others? Let them help themselves!
- Jack of ♠ — I had to cheat—I didn't have any other choices.
- 10 of ♥ — If you really liked me, you'd do what I asked.
- 10 of ♦ — That person has everything I should have.
- 10 of ♣ — They shouldn't be going to our school.
- 10 of ♠ — My job is the most important thing in my life.
- 9 of ♥ — Sex, the word that says it all.
- 9 of ♦ — I heard you like gossip! Have I got some gossip for you!
- 9 of ♣ — This would be a better place if that person weren't around.
- 9 of ♠ — You don't have to tell that person the truth. He or she will never find out.
- 8 of ♥ — You can never be rich enough.
- 8 of ♦ — Your older sister or brother really has it all together.
- 8 of ♣ — My reputation stinks. I might as well live up to it.
- 8 of ♠ — The poor don't have to be poor! They're just too lazy to work.
- 7 of ♥ — If you love me, then you'll _____.
- 7 of ♦ — Money is more important than anything.
- 7 of ♣ — Little lies are okay.
- 7 of ♠ — I don't care how they feel.
- 6 of ♥ — Everybody's doing it.
- 6 of ♦ — Family time?! Yuk!
- 6 of ♣ — I've got to be Number One.
- 6 of ♠ — Sex and drugs and rock 'n' roll!
- 5 of ♥ — What do you expect from someone like that person?
- 5 of ♦ — Parents are great when it comes to giving money, not advice.
- 5 of ♣ — The only thing good enough is straight "A"s.
- 5 of ♠ — Younger brothers and sisters are a drag. I don't need to spend time with them.
- 4 of ♥ — That person didn't really deserve to get that part, play that position, or get that grade.
- 4 of ♦ — Maybe I was wrong to say something bad about that person, but he or she started it.
- 4 of ♣ — Use 'em!
- 4 of ♠ — That person's not good enough, or smart enough, and people hate her or him.
- 3 of ♥ — That award should have been mine!
- 3 of ♦ — The only thing that's important is how it will look on my college application.
- 3 of ♣ — The world looks better when I'm high.
- 3 of ♠ — That religion stuff is a crock.
- 2 of ♥ — I lie, but sometimes you have to.
- 2 of ♦ — If you can't win, cheat!
- 2 of ♣ — I don't date ugly.
- 2 of ♠ — If you don't have the right clothes, you'll never get anywhere.

HOLY ORDERS AT THE MOVIES

ON YOUR MARK!
- To provide a springboard for a discussion of the sacrament of Holy Orders

GET SET!
- Rent the video *Romero*.
- Show the video from the party scene to the scene in which the Archbishop retrieves the Eucharist.

GO!
Ask teens to discuss these or similar questions.
- What is it in Archbishop Romero's priesthood that called him to put his life on the line?
- Who challenged him to be a better priest and bishop?
- Do the poor, the marginalized, and the left-out have a special claim on priests?
- In what ways do you see the priest or priests in your parish living out their priesthood?
- If your vocation caused you to put your life on the line, do you think you would be strong enough to live up to the challenge? Why or why not?
- What did Archbishop Romero learn from Jesus Christ? How did the Gospel shape his life?

APRIL DISCUSSION STARTER: THE MAYOR'S OFFICE

ON YOUR MARK!
To help young people:
- See the need to make moral decisions based on principles
- Develop problem-solving skills
- Understand that people are more important than things

GET SET!
- Read the scenario yourself.
- Adapt the number of roles to the size of your group. If your group is large, ask young people to form two or more groups for this activity. If your group is small, reduce the number of roles.
- Have young people choose roles to take in a discussion of the scenario.
- Read, or have a volunteer read, the scenario out loud to the group.

GO!

SCENARIO
The mayor swept into office with an unprecedented eighty-two percent of the vote. Everyone loves the mayor! Talk about Joe Popular! But now the mayor has to meet with his staff to help him through a very difficult time.

The Jewish community loves the mayor. He was given their endorsement before any other group endorsed his candidacy. He has spoken at the local synagogue, and the members campaigned hard for him. He has worked all of his life to improve Jewish-Christian relations in the community. He handpicked the deputy mayor, who is Jewish. The most likely successor to the mayor, she's very popular and competent.

Here's the mayor's challenge. A neo-Nazi group wants to hold a march right through the center of the town. They will be marching on the Jewish community's high holy day. The neo-Nazi group has a reputation for pro-Nazi statements and hateful, offensive comments about Jewish people. They need a parade permit in order to hold their march.

A civil liberties group enters the picture. They don't like the neo-Nazis any more than the mayor and others who oppose giving the group a parade permit. But they believe very strongly in the right to free speech. The mayor has always been a strong supporter of free speech, but he does not want to allow the neo-Nazis to march through the town, especially on a Jewish high holy day. He also realizes that free speech needs to be protected, even when it isn't popular.

The way he sees it, if he votes to issue the parade permit, he will be letting the Jewish community down. And if he votes not to issue the permit, he will not be living up to the principle of free speech, and the town will probably be sued by the civil liberties group.

GATHERED AT THE DISCUSSION TABLE ARE:

- The mayor
- An advisor who represents the Jewish community
- A civil liberties lawyer who does not support the racist, anti-Jewish group, but believes they have the right to free speech
- A resident of the town who doesn't want the town to have a racist image

YOUR TASK:

- Listen to all points of view and decide what is the right thing for the mayor to do.
- Convince the mayor to accept that your decision represents the best thing to do.

Notes for Group Leaders

In the *Discussion Starter*, teens take on the roles of persons involved in this situation. They are "acting" in the initial discussion.

What is most important is to bring the discussion to a conclusion. After the discussion, ask young people to shift away from their roles and return to being themselves. Help teens to process the experience by asking questions such as these:

- What values are involved in this scenario?
- What Catholic teachings can be applied?
- How are those involved in this situation called to be Christ?

Young people deserve to be so much more than actors with roles: they are disciples of Christ, learning how to take faith into the community!

MAY

MAY-AT-A-GLANCE

May is derived from the name of the goddess Maia, daughter of Atlas and mother of Hermes. The Romans considered Maia the goddess of spring.

MAY FROM A CATHOLIC CHRISTIAN PERSPECTIVE

May is traditionally the month of Mary, the Mother of God. She is Queen of the May! Traditionally, Catholics have celebrated with May Queens, May crownings, praying the rosary, and singing Marian hymns. The month of May begins with a celebration for Mary's husband, Joseph.

GREAT CHURCH FEAST DAYS

4 St. Monica (d. 387)—St. Monica, the mother of the great teacher Augustine, helped bring him from a life of wickedness to the Church. She is honored as the patron of married women and a model for all Christian mothers.

15 St. Isidore the Farmer (d. 1130)—A farm laborer, St. Isidore is a model of Christian perfection. While he worked, he conversed with God, with his guardian angel, and with the saints. He is honored as the patron of Madrid.

26 St. Philip Neri (d. 1595)—St. Philip Neri's lifework was the renewal of the faith in Rome. He began by preaching on street corners and eventually became known as "The Apostle of Rome." He is the founder of the Congregation of the Oratory.

27 St. Bede the Venerable (d. 735)—St. Bede, the only English doctor, or accomplished teacher, of the Church, is also honored for his important account of England's history.

31 St. Angela Merici (d. 1540)—As a young woman, St. Angela decided to teach children whose parents could not afford to educate them. She eventually founded the Ursulines, the first teaching order of women established in the Church. The order is named for another saint, St. Ursula, who is honored as a leader of women.

31 The Visitation of the Blessed Virgin Mary—This feast commemorates Mary's visit to her cousin Elizabeth, whose pregnancy at an advanced age is a sign that, with God, all things are possible. The story of this visit is told in Luke 1:39-56.

SAINT OF THE MONTH
St. Joseph
(First century)

St. Joseph has two feast days. On March 19, the Church celebrates Joseph, the husband of Mary. On May 1, we celebrate Joseph the Worker. Joseph is the patron of the universal Church, fathers, carpenters, social justice, and the dying. Joseph teaches us what it means to live with faith, trusting in God and relying not on our own understanding, but God's. Joseph, the carpenter, can teach us much about building the kingdom of God.

STORY ART: KITES

ON YOUR MARK!

- To provide young people with an experiential way to understand the Holy Spirit
- To encourage teens to use creativity to express their experiences of God's guidance
- To help young people reflect on the places and faces in which they have experienced God

GET SET!

- From craft catalogs or local craft stores, purchase make-it-yourself kite kits or gather the materials to create your own kits. Provide one kit for each young person and adult participating, and have a couple of extra kits on hand in case of major creative errors.
- Gather materials for decorating the kites: magazines, glue sticks, markers, colored pencils, yarn, scraps of material.
- On newsprint or on the chalkboard list the gifts and fruits of the Spirit. Gifts: wisdom, understanding, counsel, fortitude, knowledge, piety, and fear of the Lord. Fruits: charity, joy, peace, patience, kindness, goodness, generosity, gentleness, faithfulness, modesty, self-control, chastity. (See the *Catechism of the Catholic Church*, paragraphs 1831 and 1832.)
- Provide copies of **Handout 18: Story Art Directions** and **Handout 19: The Spirit in Scripture**, one for each participant.
- This activity, which would take an entire afternoon, could be done in one long session or during several sessions.

GO!

- Distribute kite kits to each participant. Invite participants to work in groups of three or four at large tables.
- Explain the process. Everyone will be making a kite. For each section of the kite, there are stories and an art project. The stories are the participants' own. The groups will be given a question to discuss and then be asked to represent that on their kites. Each member of the group should be encouraged to participate in the discussion. At this point participants will be decorating their kites. They will construct the kites later. Distribute copies of **Handout 18**.

Discussion and decorating—90 minutes
Construction and kite-flying—60 minutes
Discussion after kite-flying—20 minutes
Index card affirmation—30 to 60 minutes
Closing prayer—30 minutes

- After everyone has completed these tasks, construct the kites and take them out for their first flight. After this test flight, ask participants to discuss these or similar questions. If the weather is pleasant, hold the discussion and finish the rest of this activity in the field in which you flew the kites.

What was the best part of making these kites? What was the most difficult part?

How was this activity similar to how we experience God? (Look for comments on the importance of sharing stories, being creative, letting the wind take us, expecting and coping with ups and downs, developing the gifts and fruits of the Spirit. Encourage creativity and spontaneity in this discussion.)

- Distribute index cards of various colors. Instruct each participant to take a different colored card for each member of their small group. They will need to label one side of each card with the name of a group member. On the other side of the card, participants are to finish the following statements as they apply to the group member they chose.

I was struck by your....

Something you said that I want to think about more is....

I think you're great because....

I promise to pray for you regarding....

- When everyone has finished writing, collect the cards and give them to the teens for which they were written. Give teens time to read their cards.
- Ask participants to form a large circle, putting their kites face down in front of them. To close, ask each person to think of one thing he or she learned, felt, struggled with, or realized, and to think of a way to express that one thing in seven or fewer words. Explain that everyone will share these ideas in a closing prayer.
- Before each person shares, ask the group to say, "The Spirit moves." After each person shares, all say, "The Spirit guides. Be with us, Holy Spirit." When all are finished, recite the prayer to the Holy Spirit together:

Come, Holy Spirit, fill the hearts of your faithful.
And kindle in them the fire of your love.
Send forth your Spirit, O Lord, and our hearts shall be created.
And you shall renew the face of the earth.

If there's time, allow participants to spend some more time flying their kites.

Handout 18 — Story Art Directions

Story One: Where are some of the places and faces in which you have experienced God? Share stories about these.

Art Project One: In the center of your kite, draw a circle that touches each of the quadrants of the kite. Or draw a cross that stretches across the four quadrants. Within the outline represent the places and faces and stories you shared.

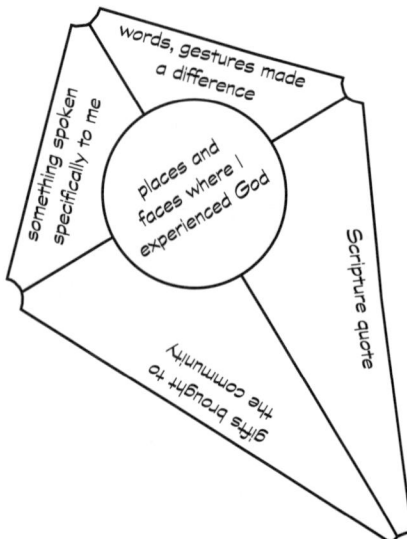

Story Two: Do you remember a moment when someone said something you really needed to hear or something that seemed to be spoken specifically to you? Or when you heard a song or read something or caught a glimpse of something that you felt really spoke to you? Share stories about these instances.

Art Project Two: On the left-hand top quadrant of your kite, represent these stories.

Story Three: Do you remember a time when you were the person who said something or did something that really made a difference to another person? You may not have even known why your words or gesture were so important to the person, but you remember the way the person reacted. Tell these stories.

Art Project Three: Represent these on the right-hand top quadrant of your kite.

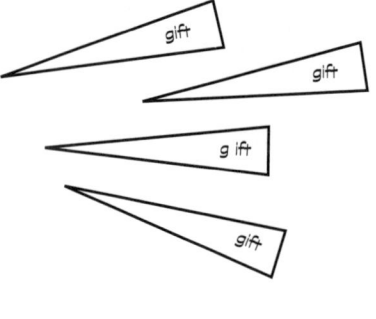

Story Four: Look at the gifts and fruits of the Spirit listed for you. Think of a person who clearly displays two or three of these traits for the good of the community. Tell some stories that show these traits.

Art Four: In the left-hand bottom quadrant, represent the gifts this person brings to the community.

Story Five: Look again at the list of gifts and fruits of the Spirit. Choose two that you feel have already become part of the way you would describe yourself. (You probably will still be perfecting them!) Also choose two that you would like to know more about and apply more fully. Share stories about these qualities.

Art Project Five: Choose four small scraps of material and cut them into long triangles. Use permanent cloth markers to put the name of the gifts or fruits on the triangles. Attach these to string, which will be the kite's tail.

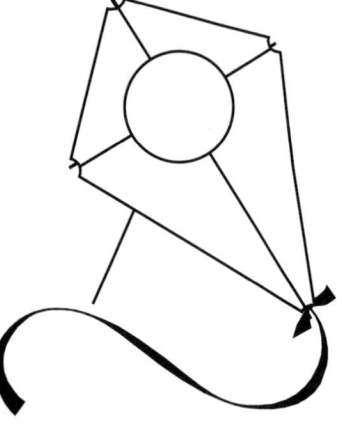

Story Six: Look at the Scripture passages on **Handout 19**. Choose a quote that you feel speaks to you right now. Share with your group why this is true.

Art Project Six: Put the entire quote, or key words from it, on the bottom right-hand quadrant of your kite.

Handout 19 🕊 The Spirit in Scripture

If we live by the Spirit, let us also be guided by the Spirit. Galatians 5:25	For all who are led by the Spirit of God are children of God. Romans 8:14
...and hope does not disappoint us, because God's love has been poured into our hearts through the Holy Spirit that has been given to us. Romans 5:5	To each is given the manifestation of the Spirit for the common good....All these are activated by one and the same Spirit, who allots to each one individually just as the Spirit chooses. 1 Corinthians 12:7, 11
Likewise the Spirit helps us in our weakness; for we do not know how to pray as we ought, but that very Spirit intercedes with sighs too deep for words. Romans 8:26	Now we have received not the spirit of the world, but the Spirit that is from God, so that we may understand the gifts bestowed on us by God. 1 Corinthians 2:12
When the Spirit of truth comes, [the Spirit] will guide you into all the truth... John 16:13	Now the Lord is the Spirit, and where the Spirit of the Lord is, there is freedom. 2 Corinthians 3:17

The Spirit of the Lord is upon me,
    because he has anointed me to bring
    good news to the poor.
Luke 4:18
	And do not grieve the Holy Spirit of God....
	Ephesians 4:30

Do not quench the Spirit. 1 Thessalonians 5:19	...for God did not give us a spirit of cowardice, but rather a spirit of power and of love and of self-discipline. 2 Timothy 1:7
But the Advocate, the Holy Spirit, whom the Father will send in my name, will teach you everything, and remind you of all that I [Jesus] have said to you. John 14:26	

VIRTUAL GOLF

ON YOUR MARK!

- To teach teens the theological and cardinal virtues
- To help teens explore Catholic virtues
- To help teens understand how the virtues relate to everyday life

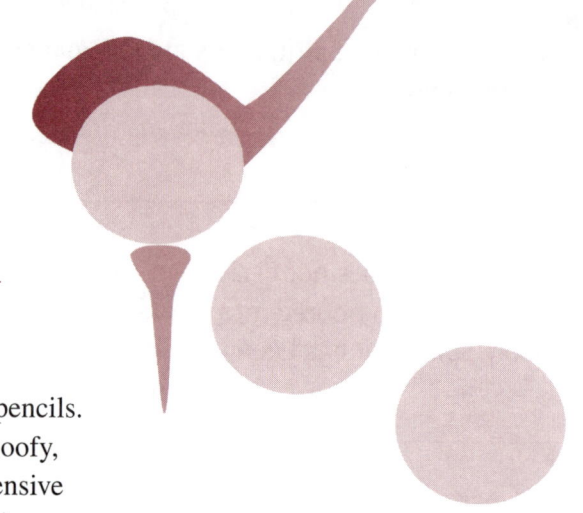

GET SET!

- Make copies of **Handout 20: Virtual Golf Scorecard**, one for each participant.
- Prepare a miniature golf course, or ask the owner of a local miniature golf course if you could use the course for an afternoon.
- Make and post signs at each of the front nine holes. Each sign should be the name of one of the virtues listed on **Handout 20**.
- Provide participants with pencils.
- Have a small, preferably goofy, prize available—an inexpensive trophy, a chocolate medallion on a ribbon, or a computer-generated certificate with a blank for writing the name of the awardee, declaring the person "Goofy Golfer of the Year."

GO!

- Explain that *virtue* comes from the word *power*. Virtue is the power to do good.
- Give each participant a scorecard (**Handout 20**) and a pencil. The participants will play nine holes of golf. If your group is large, divide the group into teams of four. Have Team One start at the first hole, Team Two at the third hole, Team Three at the fifth hole, and so on, to accommodate the size of your group.
- Before the golfers take to the course, have them review their scorecards. Ask:

  Of all the virtues listed, which do you think you have developed into the strongest? Which virtue challenges you most?

- Have teens keep score. Set a maximum number of putts per hole. For example, if someone doesn't get the ball in the hole with ten putts, that person takes a "10" for his or her score for the hole and moves on. Participants can have a stroke removed from their scores when they "max out" on a hole if they tell the leader a brief story at the end of their round about how a particular virtue has operated in their lives.
- The participant with the lowest score wins.

When the game is finished:
- Award the prize for the lowest score.
- Affirm teens' stories about how the virtues connect with their own lives.
- Encourage teens to be persons of virtue.

Handout 20 🌿 Virtual Golf Scorecard

Golfer _____

HOLE	VIRTUE	SCORE

HOLE 1 — **Theological Virtues**
The theological virtues have to do with our relationship to God. There are three theological virtues—faith, hope, and charity.
SCORE: _____

HOLE 2 — **Faith**
Someone with faith has a personal knowledge of God, believing in God and all that God has revealed.
SCORE: _____

HOLE 3 — **Hope**
The virtue of hope helps us to take responsibility for the future. Because we hope in the salvation promised by God, we work to make the world a better place, to bring about the reign of God.
SCORE: _____

HOLE 4 — **Charity or Love**
"...God is love" (1 John 4:8), and when we love God and our neighbors, we participate in the very life of God. Charity is considered the greatest virtue.
SCORE: _____

HOLE 5 — **Cardinal Virtues**
As the theological virtues help us build our relationship with God, the cardinal virtues help us in our relationships with one another.
SCORE: _____

HOLE 6 — **Prudence**
Prudence involves the ability to make the right decision at the right time. To act prudently involves discerning God's will in a situation. When we discern rather than jump to a conclusion, we slow down to think things through.
SCORE: _____

HOLE 7 — **Justice**
To achieve justice, we need to ask the question: What rights are involved in a situation and what duties are attached to those rights? You have the right to life; I have a duty to respect that right.
SCORE: _____

HOLE 8 — **Temperance**
Temperance involves moderation in all things—food, drink, sex, and so on.
SCORE: _____

HOLE 9 — **Fortitude**
Fortitude is the ability to stay calm and to act with courage. A person with great fortitude faces a life-threatening illness with quiet dignity. A person with great fortitude can lead the charge against injustice.
SCORE: _____

TOTAL _____

MAY DISCUSSION STARTER: THE LOCAL FOOTBALL TEAM

ON YOUR MARK!

To help young people:
- See the need to make decisions based on moral principles
- Develop problem-solving skills
- Understand that people are more important than things

GET SET!

- Read the scenario yourself.
- Adapt the number of roles to the size of your group. If your group is large, ask young people to form two or more groups for this activity. If your group is small, reduce the number of roles.
- Have young people choose roles to take in a discussion of the scenario.
- Read, or have a volunteer read, the scenario out loud to the group.

GO!

SCENARIO

For fourteen years, you have spent millions of dollars trying to bring an NFL championship to your hometown. People love you because you have single-handedly kept football in the city, even though you had lucrative offers to move the team to other cities. This year you have a chance at the championship. Your team is 6 and 0, the team's best record ever.

That is, until the phone wakes you at 2:15 am. You suspect that no good news ever comes at this hour, and you're right. A reporter tells you that the quarterback who helped the team to its record season has been arrested for sexual assault. You know the reporter wants you to comment, but you refuse.

You convene your top management and you gather the facts. There is no doubt that the quarterback engaged in sexual activity with the young woman who claims to have been sexually assaulted. Even his attorneys do not deny this. Their position is that the sexual activity was consensual, but this defense seems doubtful. Several witnesses have come forward to say that the victim was screaming, "No!" as she left the party with the quarterback. Witnesses go so far as to say that the player forced her to accompany him. She begged for help, but everyone froze. Finally, someone called the police. The quarterback was arrested at his home.

Your daughter is one of the witnesses who will testify against

your quarterback. You know that she and the other witnesses are telling the truth.

You have been advised by the quarterback's attorneys to do nothing. If you fire him, they say, you will prejudice the jury against him. And you'll be without your star quarterback and Super Bowl ring. The attorneys have asked you to release a statement saying, "We believe he is innocent until proven guilty. We will not act on this charge until he is tried by a jury of his peers." That will enable him to play the rest of the season, bring home the championship, and then be tried. If he's found guilty, you can fire him at that time.

Your daughter, as well as thousands of other fans, want him fired now. They feel he's guilty. You know they're right. You also know that when he was in college, he had a sexual assault charge expunged from his record. And now, other women have come forward to say that he had assaulted them. For these people, he's guilty. Case closed.

On the other hand, thousands of fans are urging you to keep the quarterback on. Their take is, Let him have his day in court. Let us have our day on the field. These people claim that what he does in his personal life has nothing to do with what he does on the field. Some remind you that Babe Ruth was sometimes drunk in public. No one said that his drinking influenced his playing.

You know that if you fire the quarterback, the season will change. Your team will have no shot at winning Super Bowl rings. It will be difficult to make payroll—you went out on the limb this year expecting to go to the Super Bowl. You know that if you fire the quarterback, you will have to pay his contract for the next six years. If you wait to fire him until after his trial and he is found guilty, you won't owe him a dime.

But as a mother, you can't help but wonder. What if your daughter had become the victim? If you don't fire the quarterback, what does this say about you and your team? Are you willing to win at any cost?

On the other hand, are you willing to face the cost of losing? Without at least a division title, you won't be able to make it financially. You will have to consider an offer to move the team. Moving the football team would demoralize the city, not to mention putting hundreds of people out of work.

GATHERED AT THE DISCUSSION TABLE ARE:
- The owner of the football team
- An attorney for the quarterback
- The owner's advisors
- The owner's daughter

YOUR TASK:
- Help the owner reach a decision about how to handle the situation involving the quarterback.

Notes for Group Leaders

In the *Discussion Starter*, teens take on the roles of persons involved in this situation. They are "acting" in the initial discussion.

What is most important is to bring the discussion to a conclusion. After the discussion, ask young people to shift away from their roles and return to being themselves. Help teens to process the experience by asking questions such as these:

- What values are involved in this scenario?
- What Catholic teachings can be applied?
- How are those involved in this situation called to be Christ?

Young people deserve to be so much more than actors with roles: they are disciples of Christ, learning how to take faith to the marketplace!

JUNE

JUNE-AT-A-GLANCE

Juno, Roman goddess and wife of the god Jupiter, gives the month of June its name. One story about Juno shows that she was jealous and acted rashly. Because she believed that Echo, who was very fond of talking, had tricked her, Juno had Echo's voice taken away. From that point forward, Echo could only reply.

JUNE FROM A CATHOLIC CHRISTIAN PERSPECTIVE

Rather than celebrating gods and goddesses who take gifts away in anger, Catholic Christians celebrate the God of life who keeps giving and giving. Depending on the date of Easter, the Ascension and Pentecost may be celebrated during the month of June. The Ascension celebrates Jesus' glorified body rising into heaven. At Pentecost, the Church celebrates the gift of the Spirit that freed the disciples.

In June, we even celebrate the ordinary with a return to Ordinary Time! Our God is an awesome God!

GREAT CHURCH FEAST DAYS

- **The Feast of the Ascension**—Celebrated on the fortieth day after Easter, this feast commemorates the ascension of Jesus' risen and glorified body into heaven.
- **Pentecost**—On the seventh Sunday after Easter, Christians celebrate the Holy Spirit's coming to the disciples and the beginning of the Church.
- **3 Sts. Charles Lwanga and Joseph Mukasa, and Companions** (d. 1886)—These Ugandan saints were killed in their ruler's attempt to eliminate Christianity among his people. After these deaths, the persecutions spread, but the number of baptisms and catechumens continued to grow.
- **10 St. Margaret of Scotland** (d. 1093)—St. Margaret influenced her husband, the king of Scotland, to works of justice, mercy, and charity.
- **13 St. Anthony of Padua** (d. 1231)—St. Anthony was a gifted preacher who attracted great numbers of people to Christianity.
- **21 St. Aloysius Gonzaga** (d. 1591)—Even though his father was determined that he become a soldier, St. Aloysius eventually achieved his goal of becoming a Jesuit. He is the patron of Catholic youth.
- **29 Sts. Peter and Paul** (first century)—It is believed that St. Peter and St. Paul were both martyred on the same day of the same year.

SAINT OF THE MONTH
John the Baptist

John the Baptist was a character! Scripture tells us that John wore "clothing of camel's hair with a leather belt around his waist, and his food was locusts and wild honey" (Matthew 3:4). He lived as a hermit in the desert and preached against the evil that was happening around him. He called for repentance and told people that the "kingdom of heaven has come near" (Matthew 3:2).

John spoke out against the adulterous marriage of Herod, the tetrarch, or ruler, of Galilee, to Herodias, who had been the wife of Herod's half-brother Philip. John was imprisoned, but Herod was reluctant to execute him. Then Herod, on the occasion of his birthday party, granted Herodias's daughter Salome one wish. After conspiring with her mother, Salome asked for the head of John the Baptist. Her wish was granted immediately.

ROCKS AND STONES

ON YOUR MARK!

- To encourage young people to think about the people who influenced them during the past academic year
- To help young people gain a greater insight into how the Scriptures speak to us

GET SET!

- Provide a small aquarium rock, or a flat black stone, for each participant.
- Ask a person who is good at crafts what can be used to write on these stones. Paint pens are readily available from craft stores and work well. White correction fluid also works well.
- Copy **Handout 21: Rocks and Stones** for the volunteer who will read it. If possible, allow this person to prepare the reading ahead of time.
- Make enough copies of the Scripture passages on **Handout 22: Rocks and Stones in Scripture** so that there will be one passage for each teen. Cut the passages apart so that each slip has one passage, and put the slips into a basket in your prayer space.

GO!

- Have a volunteer read out loud the script on **Handout 21: Rocks and Stones**. To add a little variety, suggest that the person read it as a favorite movie or cartoon character—Forrest Gump, Homer Simpson—might.
- Pass the basket of Scripture passages and ask each teen to take one and prepare to read to the group.
- Encourage teens to pay close attention to the words of sacred Scripture to see what being described as rocks and stones says about us.
- After the Scripture passages have been read, point out how rocks and stones can be positive or negative.
- Then ask each teen to take a stone. Have teens write on their stones a virtue or other good quality or action that they would like to be mindful of during the coming summer. Allow time for them to decorate their stones. Encourage teens to carry their stones as reminders of their goals.
- Close with this, or a similar, short prayer:

We come to Jesus, a living stone, rejected by human beings, but chosen and precious in the sight of God. We ask that we, like living stones, may be built into a spiritual house, where we will be a holy priesthood, offering spiritual sacrifices acceptable to God through Jesus Christ.

During his brief public ministry, John the Baptist constantly pointed to Jesus: "Here is the Lamb of God who takes away the sin of the world" (John 1:29). John also declared that he was "not worthy to untie the thong of [Jesus'] sandal" (John 1:27). When commenting on his own ministry, John spoke of Jesus and said, "He must increase, but I must decrease" (John 3:30). That's not bad advice for each of us to take in our own ministry: Jesus must increase, but we must decrease!

The Church celebrates the birth of John the Baptist on June 24.

Handout 21 ~ Rocks and Stones

We use the word *rock* in many different ways—rock solid, rock 'n' roll, rock of ages, rock concert, rock and bowl, rock-a-bye baby, and Rock on! Someone is negatively referred to as having "rocks in the head." Yet, someone can be given a supreme compliment by being told he or she is "like a rock."

We also use the word *stone* in many different ways. "He's stoned" is a bad thing. "She's stone-cold sober" is a good thing. Someone who is cold has a heart of stone. Sticks and stones can break my bones. Then there are the famed Hollywood stones: Sharon and Oliver. There are stones that we skip across the water's surface, and stones whose surfaces cause them to be sold for thousands of dollars. There's stone soup and rolling stones. Of these rolling stones, some gather no moss and some gather for concert tours. Of course, the biggest thrill imaginable is having your picture on the cover of *Rolling Stone*.

Throughout Scripture, there are many references to rocks and stones. Some are positive, some less than positive. Stones can be instruments of death, or they can be living stones. But these references tell us about our condition as human beings.

When we look at the past academic year, it is good to pause, slow down, and ask ourselves as the Scriptures are read, What kind of stones or rocks are we? How are we instruments of harm? How are we living stones?

Handout 22 — Rocks and Stones in Scripture (page 1)

Do not presume to say to yourselves, "We have Abraham as our ancestor"; for I tell you, God is able from these stones to raise up children to Abraham.
                    Matthew 3:9

And I tell you, you are Peter, and on this rock I will build my church, and the gates of Hades will not prevail against it.
                    Matthew 16:18

So they went with the guard and made the tomb secure by sealing the stone.
                    Matthew 27:66

The tempter came and said to [Jesus], "If you are the Son of God, command these stones to become loaves of bread."
                    Matthew 4:3

Jerusalem, Jerusalem, the city that kills the prophets and stones those who are sent to it! How often have I desired to gather your children together as a hen gathers her brood under her wings, and you were not willing!
                    Matthew 23:37

They had been saying to one another, "Who will roll away the stone for us from the entrance to the tomb?" When they looked up, they saw that the stone, which was very large, had already been rolled back.
                    Mark 16:3-4

Is there anyone among you who, if your child asks for bread, will give a stone?
                    Matthew 7:9

At that moment the curtain of the temple was torn in two, from top to bottom. The earth shook, and the rocks were split.
                    Matthew 27:51

He answered, "I tell you, if these were silent, the stones would shout out."
                    Luke 19:40

Everyone then who hears these words of mine and acts on them will be like a wise [one] who built [a] house on rock. The rain fell, the floods came, and the winds blew and beat on that house, but it did not fall, because it had been founded on rock.
                    Matthew 7:24-25

So Joseph took the body [of Jesus] and wrapped it in a clean linen cloth and laid it in his own new tomb, which he had hewn in the rock. He then rolled a great stone to the door of the tomb and went away.
                    Matthew 27:59-60

Now standing there were six stone water jars for the Jewish rites of purification, each holding twenty to thirty gallons.
                    John 2:6

Handout 22   Rocks and Stones in Scripture (page 2)

Now in the law Moses commanded us to stone such women. Now what do you say?
John 8:5

The disciples said to him, "Rabbi, the Jews were just now trying to stone you, and are you going there again?"
John 11:8

Early on the first day of the week, while it was still dark, Mary Magdalene came to the tomb and saw the stone had been removed from the tomb.
John 20:1

When they kept on questioning him, he straightened up and said to them, "Let anyone among you who is without sin be the first to throw a stone at her."
John 8:7

Then Jesus, again greatly disturbed, came to the tomb. It was a cave, and a stone was lying against it. Jesus said, "Take away the stone." Martha, the sister of the dead man, said to him, "Lord, already there is a stench because he has been dead four days."
John 11:38-39

Then they dragged him out of the city and began to stone him; and the witnesses laid their coats at the feet of a young man named Saul.
Acts 7:58

So they picked up stones to throw at him, but Jesus hid himself and went out of the temple.
John 8:59

So they took away the stone. And Jesus looked upward and said, "Father, I thank you for having heard me."
John 11:41

…And all drank the same spiritual drink. For they drank from the spiritual rock that followed them, and the rock was the Christ.
1 Corinthians 10:4

The Jews took up stones again to stone him. Jesus replied, "I have shown you many good works from the Father. For which of these are you going to stone me?"
John 10:31-32

When Pilate heard these words, he brought Jesus outside and sat on the judge's bench at a place called The Stone Pavement, or in Hebrew Gabbatha.
John 19:13

…And you show that you are a letter of Christ, prepared by us, written not with ink but with the Spirit of the living God, not on tablets of stone but on tablets of human hearts.
2 Corinthians 3:3

A GUIDED MEDITATION ON RELATIONSHIPS

ON YOUR MARK!

- To give teens an opportunity to pause and look at their relationships with Jesus and with others

GET SET!

- Prepare a prayer space. Cover a small table with an attractive cloth. Decorate the table with a candle, crucifix, and some brightly colored flowers.
- Explain that this prayer will be a guided meditation, for which young people will need to relax and to use their imaginations. Invite young people to make themselves comfortable, either in their chairs or on the floor. You may choose to play some soft instrumental music. To prevent distractions, try not to use music teens are likely to recognize.
- Invite young people to close their eyes and quiet their minds.

GO!

- Read the script on **Handout 23: A Guided Meditation on Relationships**, speaking slowly and pausing where appropriate.

Handout 23 — A Guided Meditation on Relationships (page 1)

Respond to the following meditation to the degree with which you are comfortable. Relax your body and take deep breaths. Breathe in. Hold the breath. Breathe out. Breathe in. Hold the breath. Breathe out slowly. Let go of the tension in your body and just relax. Relax your feet and your legs. Relax. Make a fist. Clench the fist. Release the fist. Relax. Tighten your arm and shoulder muscles. Release the muscles. Relax. Relax your stomach and breathe deeply. Let go of the tensions in your neck, your face, your forehead, your eyes. Slowly let all the tension flow out of your body. Breathe in deeply. Hold the breath. Breathe out slowly. Relax. Now imagine:

You are walking through the countryside on a picture-perfect day. The wind is gently ruffling your hair and clothing. This is one of those days when you are happy to be alive. Everything is perfect. Take a moment to notice your surroundings and your feelings.

Pause.

In the distance, you see a blur of colors—bright, rich, wonderful colors moving with the soft wind. You walk closer to investigate and see that you are approaching a garden. As you draw near, you see a garden that has been well cultivated, well cared for, and well loved. Look around the garden.

Pause.

There is little evidence of the things that can ruin a garden. No signs of decay, insects, rodents. No, this garden is perfect.

You sit down in front of the garden for a while—happy to relax and happier still to soak in the smells, the sights, the beauty of this garden. Reds, greens, yellows, and purples dot this amazing plot of land. How wonderfully well this garden has been cared for!

Peace comes over you. Peace and calm fill you. Nothing and everything is on your mind.

Pause.

So at peace are you that it takes you by surprise to learn that someone has approached and is sitting next to you. The Gardener! You want to find the words that describe your feelings about the Gardener's work. You want to tell the Gardener that this is the most beautiful spot you have ever seen. But words fail. You feel it is better to be silent in the presence of such beauty. The Gardener seems to understand how you are feeling. He smiles and nods. You know that you are being encouraged to be still, to stay silent. The two of you look at the garden.

Pause.

You feel the Gardener's hand on your shoulder. You turn to look at the Gardener and say, "I just want to thank you."

Handout 23   A Guided Meditation on Relationships (page 2)

The Gardener smiles and says, "I just want to thank you, too. I have watched you tend the garden of your life, and you have been a faithful gardener. You have nourished friends with the warmth of your smile. You have tended to their needs with care. When you saw someone who needed extra attention, you gave it. When someone had been bruised along the way, you fed that one with extra love, bringing the person back to full health."

You pause, thinking about your own relationships. In your mind, you see the people in your life, each with his or her own beauty and style. What do you see when you look at the relationships that make up the garden of your life?

Pause.

After looking at the beauty of the garden, you begin to notice areas of your relationship garden that show signs of a lack of attention. You may have neglected or trampled on a few plants. Pause to think about aspects of the relationships that need your attention.

Pause.

You feel the Gardener's hand on your shoulder again. In that moment, you know that even the areas of your relationship garden that need work are not beyond your ability to repair with the Gardener's help. The Gardener embraces you. It is time to get up. The Gardener moves among the plants and colors of the beautiful garden, and you walk arm in arm with the Gardener. Is there anything new that you notice?

Pause.

As you look at the garden, reflect one more time on the garden of your relationships.

Pause.

You realize that there is one more relationship that you want to work on—your relationship with the Gardener.

Pause.

The Gardener continues further into the garden. Soaking in one last look at the beauty, you watch as the Gardener moves on.

Pause.

Breathe in deeply. Hold the breath. Breathe out slowly. Let the image of the garden fade in your memory. When you are ready, open your eyes and come back to this moment. We close in prayer:

Gentle and loving God, You are the Gardener of our lives. As we gather, keep us mindful of one another. Let us care for one another with gentleness, compassion, and joy.

Bless us, and let us be a blessing to one another. We ask this as we ask all things, through Christ our Lord. Amen

JUNE DISCUSSION STARTER: THE D.U.I. ARREST

ON YOUR MARK!

To help young people:
- See the need to make decisions based on moral principles
- Develop problem-solving skills
- Understand that people are more important than things

GET SET!

- Read the scenario yourself.
- Adapt the number of roles to the size of your group. If your group is large, ask young people to form two or more groups for this activity. If your group is small, reduce the number of roles.
- Have young people choose roles to take in a discussion of the scenario.
- Read, or have a volunteer read, the scenario out loud to the group.

GO!

SCENARIO

Officer Smith was feeling pretty good as her 11:00 pm to 7:00 am shift began. Just the day before, she had taken the sergeant's exam, and she was sure that she had aced it. She had known the answer to every question. She was looking forward to being promoted.

As she was driving along, Officer Smith noticed a car weaving back and forth across the road in front of her. She pulled the car over and tried to speak with the driver. He reeked of alcohol and was slurring his words so, she administered a Breathalyzer test. His alcohol level was over the legal limit.

The driver told Officer Smith that he was the police commissioner's stepson. He admitted that this was the third time he had been stopped for driving under the influence. He bragged that the other two cops had let him go and implied that if she knew what was good for her career, she would, too. She decided to arrest him.

A couple of days later, a representative from the police department visited Officer Smith at her home. He told her that if she said she forgot to read the commissioner's stepson his rights, or if she chose not to appear in court on the day of the trial, then the case would be thrown out. Either of these actions would be considered a professional courtesy to the commissioner, and one he was sure not to forget. Officer Smith's promotion to sergeant would be assured. In return, the commissioner would offer his assurance that his son would go in for rehab.

Officer Smith hesitated. Her promotion was important to her. Being a cop was all she ever wanted. But she had recently called on the parents of a teenage girl who had been killed by a drunk driver. The memory of that visit was vivid. She knew that both times this young man had been picked up, he had promised to go into rehab. But he never seemed to get there.

GATHERED AROUND THIS DISCUSSION TABLE ARE:

- Officer Smith
- Two members of Officer Smith's family
- A lawyer from the Legal Aid Society
- Another police officer

YOUR TASK:

- Give Officer Smith your best advice about what she should do.

Notes for Group Leaders

In the **Discussion Starter**, teens take on the roles of persons involved in this situation. They are "acting" in the initial discussion.

What is most important is to bring the discussion to a conclusion. After the discussion, ask young people to shift away from their roles and return to being themselves. Help teens to process the experience by asking questions such as these:

- What values are involved in this scenario?
- What Catholic teachings can be applied?
- How are those involved in this situation called to be Christ?

Young people deserve to be so much more than actors with roles: they are disciples of Christ, learning how to take faith into the workplace!

More Youth Ministry Resources from Pflaum Publishing Group

New!

Activities for Teens
77 Ways to Build Catholic Identity

Energize your meetings with teens—and energize their faith at the same time! Designed to grab and hold teens' attention, these activities help teens to grow in Catholic identity and to develop problem-solving and decision-making skills. You'll find fresh ideas for each month, September to June.

Product #3214, $19.95

Retreats for Teens
Planning Strategies and Teen-Tested Models

Make retreats and days of reflection meaningful and memorable for teens. Whether you have half of a day or a full weekend, you'll find a successful working model to use "as is" or to adapt to your situation.

Product #3213, $19.95

Service Projects for Teens
20 Plans That Work

Keep teens "moving and doing" (and doing good) with these proven, hands-on Christian service projects! Each model in this collection of teen-oriented, active service projects provides the inspiration and practical direction you'll need to organize and implement each project.

Product #3215, $19.95

Pflaum Publishing Group • Dayton, OH 45439 • 800-543-4383 • www.pflaum.com

Getting Started
100 Icebreakers for Youth Gatherings

Help young people get comfortable with one another, facilitate sharing and discussion, and build a sense of community—while having a lot of fun! For each tested strategy, there's a purpose statement, time requirement, list of supplies, directions, and suggestions for adapting to different groups and settings.

Product #3211, $19.95

Making Connections
25 Stories for Sharing Faith with Teens

Initiate and guide meaningful discussion by teens on a wide choice of current topics. Reproducible stories and discussion questions promote journaling and allow teens to connect to their own experience and to their faith life.

Product #3212, $19.95

Prayer Services for Teens
34 Resources for Special Reasons and Church Seasons

Let teens lead their peers in prayer: these simple, yet powerful, prayer services make it work! Themes revolve around Feast Days and Holidays, Advent and Lent, and Life Circumstances.

Product #3210, $19.95

Save 15% on a set of all 6 titles:
Only **$99.95!**
(#3216)

Pflaum Publishing Group • Dayton, OH 45439 • 800-543-4383 • www.pflaum.com   SHB0